Entrepreneurial Thinking

How Thinking Like an Entrepreneur Can Help You "Win At Life"

ED CAWLEY

PAGE
SOLUTIONS

Page Solutions - Prowriters Network
541 Buttermilk Pike
Crescent Springs, KY 41017

ISBN 979-8-89633-035-6 (softcover)
ISBN 979-8-89633-090-5 (hardcover)
ISBN 979-8-89633-036-3 (ebook)

Printed in the United States of America.

Contents

Preface

I have spent thousands of hours reading books, articles, and other information about personal development, motivation and self-help ideas and concepts. I thought about what these so-called gurus were talking about. However, I realized that all of these approaches were missing some of what I considered to be fundamental tenants of what was needed for a person to survive and succeed in a 21st Century civilized society.

Basically, I had an AHA moment. It dawned on me that the keys to success in all areas of life are the same keys to success in business. As a fairly successful entrepreneur, myself, I realized that the mindset that helped me to succeed was very similar to how I made good in all areas of my life. I concluded that one has to **Think Like An Entrepreneur** not only in order to be successful in business but also, to be successful in all areas of their life.

This same ways of setting goals, of doing things when they need to be done, and other ways of thinking like an entrepreneur will help everyone become successful in all areas of their life. These lifetime goals include personal and professional success, personal finance, self-improvement, better health, improved personal relationships, increased creative pursuits, and more. The habits we follow and the thoughts we have on a daily basis are who we are. By changing our habits and changing the way we think, we can change our lives. Basically, if you change your mind, you will change your life. Ultimately, **Entrepreneurial Thinking** can help you "**Win At Life**" by helping you reach that next level of success, income, joy, and happiness, that you desire.

This book contains an extraordinary set of positive recommendations that can help everyone who reads it to improve their self-respect as well as most of their hopes for their future. These positive concepts also explain how it can be better to focus on **Thinking Like An Entrepreneur** to improve all aspects of your life.

Introduction

This book is divided up into 10 chapters in order to clarify how **Entrepreneurial Thinking** can improve every aspect of your life and help you **Win At Life**. First of all, you need to **Focus on Success** in all areas of your life. In order to be able to focus on success, you will need to become more financially sound. Therefore, you will need to **Improve your Finances**. One way that many people use to improve their finances is to learn **How To Make Money In Real Estate**.

As you take the steps to focus on success in other areas of your life, one of the first concepts you need to address is to **Become More Self-Aware.** As it states in this chapter, "Only if you accept who you are, can you take the steps necessary to improve yourself." Becoming more self-aware is the direct path towards what mental health professionals call Self-Actualization.

Since the concept of this book is to help you improve all aspects of your life, you also need to be aware of the importance of how to **Make Better Choices** in all areas of your life. If you **Learn How To Do Some Things Yourself,** it will become easier for you to make the decision whether or not you should do a specific task yourself or hire someone else to do it for you. As a major caveat states in this chapter, "Learn when it is time to call an expert before you destroy anything beyond repair."

The choices you make and the mindset you develop to take steps to improve yourself every day will allow you to **Improve Your Health** and to **Improve your Relationships.** Along the way, you can **Embrace Your Creativity,** Also, by understanding that **Taking The High Road Is Being Ethical,** you will finalize your progress into an **Entrepreneurial Thinking** mindset that can help you **Win At Life.**

Now I would like to present to you:

Entrepreneurial Thinking

How Thinking Like an Entrepreneur Can Help You "WIn At Life."

Summary

A true winner isn't necessarily someone who does something better than someone else. A true winner is someone who does something better today than they did yesterday. To "**Win At Life**" one needs to improve themselves in everything they do, every day, in every way possible.

Everyone needs to work on becoming the best version of ourselves. Life is a journey not a destination. To "**Win At Life**" one needs to become the best version of themselves that will consistently succeed as they travel through their journey of life.

The underlying philosophy of everything in this book is respect, courtesy, and consideration. Show respect for yourself and others. Treat everyone with the same courtesy you would like to be shown. Also with every decision, be considerate of the feelings of others that your decision might affect.

Underlying these philosophies are the main principal of what I call the "**Diamond Rule**." The "**Diamond Rule**" goes way beyond the "**Golden Rule**." Everyone understands that the "**Golden Rule**" is to always treat others the way you want to be treated. However, the "**Diamond Rule**" is to always treat others the way **THEY** want to be treated.

As a simple explanation, consider the waiter who brings a customer the waiter's favorite meal instead of what the customer ordered. The customer ordered a salad and seafood. The waiter's favorite meal is soup and steak so he brought the customer soup and steak. That is treating others the way he, himself, wanted to be treated. However, the customer actually wanted what the customer ordered, not what the waiter brought him. Obviously, using the "Golden Rule" in this and other similar situations is **NOT** the best way to behave.

Treating others, the way they want to be treated is obviously a better way to behave; however, it is not always easy to do. It requires knowing enough about the other person to make the correct choices for them. This means you must communicate well enough to truly understand what is important to the other people you are dealing with.

The following precepts, concepts, and ideas should be used as a set of guidelines that will help you, the reader, identify, develop, and make permanent the type of. thinking that will help you "**Win At Life**". **This is Entrepreneurial Thinking.**

What exactly is **Entrepreneurial Thinking**? It's not just about starting a business. To put it simply, **Entrepreneurial Thinking** is a mindset, or a specific way of thinking about everything in your life. You can **Think Like an Entrepreneur** even if you work for someone else.

Here are the basics of the **Entrepreneurial** mindset:

1. Invest your time and money in yourself first.

2. Overcome all personal challenges

3. Make things happen yourself

4. Become a student and a mentor

5. Manage your cash flow

6. Focus on growth

7. Empower others to help

8. Multiply distribution to increase income.

The **Entrepreneurial** mindset is quite different from an employee mindset. Here are the basics of what can be considered the employee mindset:

1. Wonder what do I get from my employer

2. Learn how to find my benefits?

3. Look for my problems

4. Expect someone else to solve my problems

5. Wait to be told what to do

6. Don't train a replacement

7. Wait for my paycheck

8. Only Focus on completing assigned tasks

9. Live paycheck to paycheck

Many companies encourage independent thinking using the term "intrapreneurial" or an individual within a large firm, who uses entrepreneurial skills. These individuals will work without incurring either the risks or benefits associated with their activities. Highly successful entrepreneurs make their own luck by thinking Outside the Box with clear goals, sky high expectations, and unshakable self-confidence.

Entrepreneurial Thinking helps people to learn how to expect the unexpected and visualize opportunities. They become adaptable, flexible, and able to improvise when necessary. Entrepreneurs just think and do things differently.

No one is born with all of these sterling abilities. Each piece of the human puzzle that creates a highly successful entrepreneur must be identified, developed, and made a permanent part of the entrepreneurs' daily life.

To **Think Like An Entrepreneur**, one needs to think about risk versus reward, cost versus benefit and opportunity costs. In any decision or action in your life there are always benefits and costs. The costs include the costs of alternate choices what are called opportunity costs.

For example, in its most basic form, simply waking up in the morning begins the process: what to do? what to do? Should I get up or stay in bed? Most of us feel that simply staying in bed is safe while going out into the world is risky.

That is, of course, provided that while you were in your bed a hurricane did not blow a tree through your bedroom and crush you while you slept. This is an extreme example, but it has happened in the past.

However, most of us perceive that staying in bed is safe. Once we get up, then we have to face the real world.

Now begins the choices. Each choice has a consequence. Also, each choice that takes time or other resources precludes the opportunity of using those same resources to make an alternative choice.

These opportunity costs should always be considered when making any decision. What are the benefits of getting up? Once up, maybe you can get started in a new business or you can at least get to work on time.

What are the risks? If you're late for work again you might get fired. If you start that new business, you have to have made a workable plan with clear enough goals and action steps to make yourself successful.

What about other choices? What should you have for breakfast? Should you eat sugary cereal which could lead to diabetes or a whole wheat bagel? Should you have eggs and bacon? How should you decide? The choices you make every day can and will affect your future.

As you go through your day you will be faced with hundreds, perhaps thousands of choices. If you are living with a partner, you will have to choose how to relate to your significant other before one or the other of you leaves the house. You will have to choose how to respond to your children, if you have any living with you.

If you commute, you have choices to make as to how you should interact with other commuters. Basically, you will have to choose how to act in response to every external interaction that occurs. You cannot control any external factors that you might encounter, but you can and must control your reactions to them.

You need to choose to be proactive as much as possible in order to minimize any potential negative reactions to situations beyond your control. You will also have to choose how to respond to your own thoughts, fears, and concerns as you go through the process of living from day to day.

Winning at life can be summed up with the idea of becoming a better person today than you were yesterday. The only constant in life is change. You can either change or be left behind. Just follow these guidelines and the change will always be for the better.

You need to comprehend that you are your own answer to your own path to the future and your own light along the way. This way, you are transforming what the world sends to you into your own perspective.

Life is all about choices and as you learn to cope with all of the possible consequences of choices that you make, you will begin to understand how **Entrepreneurial Thinking** can help you "**Win At Life**." The primary focus on choosing correctly is to always do the right thing at the right time for the right reason for everyone involved in your choices.

Acknowledgements

I would like to thank my wife, Florence Cawley who has always encouraged me to indulge my creativity, whether it is performing on stage in Community Theater, writing music, playing my guitar, or writing one of the several books and plays I have started but never finished.

Also, since she was a High School English Teacher for over 35 years, I have depended upon her for making sure that I did not make any grammatical errors. Her editing abilities have been essential in the format and structure of this book.

Chapter One

Focus On Success

Success is its own reward.

Appreciate your own achievements without feeling the necessity of the applause of others. You should be able to look at your own handiwork with quiet pride and a sense of accomplishment.

Although it does make you feel good when other people honor you for your success, you need to be able to feel praiseworthy for yourself without any kind of arrogance or conceit.

Also, succeeding in anything you accomplish will improve your self-respect.

Success requires focused action.

In your own personal success story, determination and perseverance are more important than intelligence and great ideas. Mensa is the largest high IQ society in the world. Your IQ has to be in the top 2% in order to be a member.

Mensa members run the gamut from college professors, research scientists, truck drivers, and laborers. Everyone is smart, but not everyone is a billionaire. Obviously, pure intelligence as the only aptitude is not the perfect yellow brick road to riches.

Million-dollar ideas abound, but great ideas are worthless without the massive, focused action it will take to make them work. To be successful you will need to make a plan and take the necessary steps in the correct sequence in order to accomplish your goal.

Entrepreneurial Thinking requires the understanding that what you do on an everyday consistent basis is the methodology for you to become successful in everything you do.

As you continue reading, you will begin to understand the structure and methodology of tasks that will enable you to accomplish every goal that is important. These goals that you focus on need to include everything that is important to you in all areas of your life.

If you want to become successful, you need to work harder than unsuccessful people.

You need to understand the 80/20 rule. Twenty percent of the people make eighty percent of the money because they get up earlier, work harder, work smarter, and try hard enough to succeed. Eighty percent of the people only make twenty percent of the money simply because they don't get up earlier, don't work harder, don't work smarter and simply don't try hard enough to succeed.

To be financially successful, you will need to make the decision to be in the top earning twenty percent group and take the steps necessary to accomplish it.

The will to win cannot be taught but it can be learned. People who engage in **Entrepreneurial Thinking** want four things in every aspect of their life. (1) They want to choose how best to spend their time. (2) They want to control how best to achieve their goals. (3) They want to work in an endeavor they believe in. (4) They want to be a part of something significant that is bigger than themselves.

The key is to finish what you start. Ernest Hemmingway said, "Finishing is what you have to do. If you don't finish, nothing is worth a Damn."

Change in your life is necessary. Winston Churchill, said "To improve is to change, so to be perfect is to change often."

Learn what you can control.

You can control your attitude. You can control your responses to external factors. You can control your work ethic. What you can't control doesn't really matter. Learn to embrace your challenges. You want difficulties. The only people that have no worries are 6 feet down or their ashes are in a chalice in a family member's home. You want bigger problems so that you can find bigger solutions that will improve your life.

You don't want to stress over the small stuff. Ignore the idiot who cut you off in traffic. Tip the rude waiter anyway. You want to worry about bigger things that are important to you. Like, "How can I make $100,000 this month?"; or "What can I do to help my team become more productive?"; Or any of the hundreds of other things that you can focus on that will make your life better.

As always, **Thinking like an Entrepreneur**, will consistently help you to make better decisions that can help you **Win At Life**.

Set goals for everything you want to accomplish.

There are two types of people in the world; those who set goals and those who don't. People who don't set goals frequently work for those who do.

Goals must be specific and measurable. Two critical characteristics of a specific, measurable goal are a quantity and a time frame. A money goal must have an amount and a date. I'm going to make a million dollars within the next 12 months. That is a goal! However, in order for a goal to be doable, it must be able to be broken down into action steps. Clearly the goal of making a million dollars in 12 months would require more than one thing to do. There is an adage that says "Success by the Yard is hard; by the inch, it's a cinch."

Some goals may be very simple. "I'm going to buy a pair of shoes." Even this has steps that must be accomplished. You must choose to buy online or go to a store. If you decide to purchase online, you need to choose an online store. If you choose to go to a brick and mortar store, you have to pick a method of transportation. Either way you will have to choose the style of shoe, pick a size, and select a method of payment.

Other goals will be far more complicated and will require many, many more action steps to accomplish them. The key is to keep the steps relatively simple and be consistent. As you go through the steps to complete a specific goal, be sure to evaluate your progress as you continue to accomplish the tasks to complete the goal.

Back in the 1960s, a man from France named Michael Lotito decided to eat a Cessna aircraft. He cut it up and melted it down into bite sized pieces and ate it. It took him a while, but he was determined and finally succeeded. Before his death in 2007, Mr. Lotito also ate 18 bicycles, 15 supermarket carts and a lot of other weird stuff.

You might not want to eat anything this strange. However, this is the perfect example of taking a huge goal and cutting it down into small doable tasks. Small doable tasks could also be called bite-sized pieces. Just make sure that the bite-sized pieces of your project don't cause you significant indigestion. 😊

Be ready to use your abilities and take the plunge into entrepreneurship when you believe it to be the right time to do so.

The plunge into entrepreneurship is a personal decision. First you need to develop the mindset of an entrepreneur.

One of the first things is for you to discover your individual "Why?" Why is it important for you to become a successful entrepreneur? It's probably not just the money. Money is just a tool. It's probably what the money can potentially do for you, your family, and perhaps the legacy you wish to leave behind.

Make a list of your "Whys?" Don't stop with the obvious, but keep going until you have a clear understanding of your "Why". To figure out your true "Why" start with the basic "Why do you want to be financially successful?" Ok, you want to earn a lot of money. Now you must answer "Why is it really important to you to earn a lot of money?"

Once you answer that question, ask the next question with "Why is it important to you to (Whatever the last answer was.) Keep going at least 7 levels deep.

It is only with a significant "Why" will you take the steps to become a truly successful entrepreneur. Your "Why" will get you up early and keep you going when the going gets tough.

You must keep your attitude positive no matter what happens. You must engage in long-term thinking rather than immediate gratification and be persistent. You must focus on the outcomes you desire and move towards these results with laser-sharp focus.

If you are coachable and consistent, you will develop the confidence to succeed against all odds. This is especially true if the person who is coaching you is a very successful entrepreneur.

The first step of **Entrepreneurial Thinking** that will help you succeed in a new business is to create a business plan. You need to start out with specific goals. The business plan should clearly demonstrate the viability of your business to generate revenue and make a profit.

Significantly, you need to consider your **S**trengths, **W**eaknesses, **O**pportunities, and **T**hreats related to business competition. This so-called **SWOT** analysis will help you create specific action items that will enable you to move towards your goals. It will also help you develop the specific skillset that is necessary to be successful in the exact entrepreneurial enterprise you have chosen.

Critical to your business plan will be several logical items that will make or break your new business. You must consider your startup costs and revenue projections ahead of time. Additionally, your action items towards your goals should include manageable tasks with specific deadlines.

To consistently move forward on a daily basis you must create a fixed routine that will help you accomplish all you need to do. Jeff Bezos says that he has a daily routine including the time he tends to sleep as well as time to perform his daily activities. A fixed routine also implies that you have a specific method to master your time management.

Having the **Mindset of an Entrepreneur** is critical to succeeding as an entrepreneur. However, without the skillset in the business you perceive to be the best opportunity to pursue, you will flounder.

Imagine someone who wants to be a mountain climber. Even with the best possible desire and even with the mindset to accomplish the task of climbing the mountain, a person who has no training in climbing skills will most likely lead to an unexpected rapid descent onto the valley floor with dire consequences. It's never the fall that kills you, it's the sudden impact of landing at the bottom.

Be the kind of leader you would want to follow. – Leadership 101

Perhaps the single most critical aspect of leadership is the positive attitude and the commitment to the business that you, as its leader demonstrate every day. Even if you become frustrated or disillusioned, your team should never know about it.

The principal of bad up and good down should be stringently followed every day. If there are any negative concepts or thoughts about the system you are engaged in, it is best to send these negative items up the organization ladder to try to change those circumstances. Meanwhile only send positive comments and encouragement down to your team.

As a leader you should always expect more of yourself than you expect of others. You should never use financial or physical advantage to demean others.

You should never ask someone else to do something you would not do yourself if you were capable to do that specific task yourself.

You need to catch other people doing the right thing. Give them praise and encouragement. A "Thank you" costs you nothing.

No matter what, treat people the way you want to be treated, or even better, treat them the way **THEY** want to be treated. You can run an organization by intimidating your teammates and acting selfishly just so long. Eventually, they will figure you out. In the comic strip "Blondie" her husband, Dagwood figured his boss, Mr. Dithers out a long time ago.

Mr. Dithers is a typical petty tyrant. He is always threatening to fire Dagwood. Even when Dagwood does an assignment well, Mr. Dithers has something negative to say. He says things like, "You did a great job so I won't fire you today. Your reward for a job well done is you get to come back to work tomorrow and get paid on payday."

As a result of these continuous negative comments from his boss, Dagwood cheats his boss nearly every day. Dagwood sleeps on the job, wastes time by hanging out at the water cooler, and does everything he can to be unproductive. This behavior is called passive-aggressive and is an employees' ways of getting back at the organization for perceived unfair treatment.

No matter how effective your product or how wonderful the service you perform for your clients is, without motivated, happy people working in your business, the ongoing success of your business is questionable. Your people, your team, are the most important factor in creating a successful organization or profitable business.

Never think of how you should "Manage" your team. You manage tasks. That's why you create "to-do" lists. You lead people. You must lead from the front; you can't push a string from behind.

One of the greatest leaders in history was Alexander the Great. He always led his army into battle from the front of the charge. This magnificent bravery made his troops follow him with great respect and admiration. By leading from the front, he earned the loyalty and devotion of his troops.

If you want to figure out whether or not you are a successful leader, look behind and see if anyone is following you. Successful leaders do what is best for their team first.

If you're in middle management, go to bat for your team. They will respect you for looking out for them and will reward you with loyalty.

By respecting every member of your team and making an effort to understand them, they will, in turn, respect you. Understanding your team members includes learning about them and their families. Learn the name of the spouse and children, if any, and the dates of special occasions such as birthdays and anniversaries. Basically, if you treat your team members similar to your own beloved family members, they will respect you very much.

Getting the respect of your team is of paramount importance. You cannot survive if your team consistently tries to undermine you due to a lack of respect and belief. If your team believes in you and respects you, then you can accomplish anything.

The easiest and most effective method of leadership is to recognize and praise your team members. Recognition of accomplishments encourages people to work harder and be more productive.

Think about yourself as a child when you brought home that first-grade work of art to your Mom. You knew that it really wasn't very good, but your Mom praised your effort and posted it in the family place of honor on the front of the refrigerator. You were so proud of yourself that you almost burst with pride.

Then how much harder did you try to do better? You tried and tried. You took more time and practiced. Eventually, you produced a drawing that even a casual onlooker could actually tell what it was a drawing of. Everyone has the need for genuine appreciation, regardless of their age.

Now think about the time when you tried something else and maybe showed your results to a less enlightened relative or friend. Their response of "How could you be so stupid; this is a piece of junk! You'll never be any good at anything!" You felt hurt. Aside from perhaps getting angry at the other person, you also felt inferior, frustrated, and unwilling to try again.

Think about yourself. Are you nurturing, caring, and able to instill a greater desire to be more productive into your team? Or do your criticisms discourage your team and cause them to be less productive? Again, you should always treat people at least the way you want to be treated or even better, the way they want to be treated.

One caveat, however, the praise and recognition must be warranted. Empty praise cheapens the recognition and insults the recipient. People aren't stupid and are well aware of whether or not they deserve recognition or criticism.

Having said that, however, think about this. Assume that your team members are used to getting well-deserved praise when they perform something the way they should. Nevertheless, perhaps the worst criticism that they can feel is to be excluded from the praise they deserve to get even though they are still doing the same thing.

This lack of deserved and expected praise can be interpreted as criticism especially if they see others getting the public recognition that they used to get but now aren't getting if for some unknown reason.

Thus, make sure that you consistently praise everyone on your team when they all have earned the praise. Praise should be given equally to all for a job well done.

Listen to the opinions of others.

Listen to other people, but do not be gullible or blindly follow anyone else's advice. You should carefully consider all options and make a rational decision.

Before you follow any advice, you need to make sure that the advice you have received corresponds with your life goals and is in line with your personal belief system. However, you must be open to the distinct possibility that someone else actually knows more about the subject than you do.

If possible, try to get the opinion of someone who has successfully accomplished what you are trying to do. Opinions of people who failed at what you are trying to accomplish are irrelevant.

Some people, especially those who are not successful in their own life, could have rock-solid opinions of why whatever you are trying to accomplish won't work. Listen to them politely but ignore what they say.

Unsuccessful people tend to want others to also be unsuccessful. Misery loves company; unsuccessful people like to bond with other unsuccessful people. That way, they will feel like their personal lack of success has nothing to do with their consistent lack of effort.

Another tenant of **Entrepreneurial Thinking** is to focus on your own success with extreme self-confidence and move forward toward your goals. Avoid the nay-sayers.

Never be jealous of someone else's success.

You have the same number of hours in a day, week, month, or year as every other person on earth.

Learn how the successful person became successful. Imitate them to become successful yourself, but never lose who you are. Besides, it might be that they are not as successful as they seem to be.

They could be like the guy in a commercial I saw once. He was talking to the camera and said something like, "Man, I'm really living the American Dream. I've got a fantastic house and two luxury cars in the garage. I'm in debt up to my eyeballs."

Obviously, his success was an illusion because he was living way beyond his means. In other words, with any slight glitch in his income, either loss of his job or an investment that went wrong, he could lose everything.

Another possibility is that other people's success could have cost them something else that you consider more valuable. Their financial success may have cost them all of their family relationships.

Some individuals spend all of their time pursuing business goals, that keep them away from home. Since they are not home, their family might find someone else to care for them. Such a loss of family may not be something you would want to give up, even for fame or fortune

Thinking like a true Entrepreneur means that you understand the importance of balancing your life. By doing so, you can improve all aspects of your life including business and personal facets.

Success is the best revenge.

As you go through life, at some point, you will most likely be the object of unfair treatments by others at least once if not multiple times. It is not legally or socially acceptable to assassinate anyone. However, despite having being treated unfairly in your former workplace, you can remove yourself from the situation and become successful in a different endeavor.

Just don't let the situation define you. If you are honest with yourself, then you are who you believe yourself to be. You are not who the negative opinions of other people say you are.

The adage that if one door closes, another one opens is true. However, you have to recognize the opening door and be willing to choose a different path if you need to. Sometimes opportunity knocks very softly and you have to listen carefully or you might miss it.

Were you unfairly terminated from a job? Consider it to be an opportunity to find a better job that serves your higher purpose. It could be a chance to find a job that makes your heart sing because you feel better about what you do on a daily basis. Or, it could be the time to take the plunge into true entrepreneurship.

As an employee, Walt Disney's first successful cartoon character was Oswald the Rabbit. The company he worked for simply paid him a salary but refused to give him the copyright to the creation of Oswald and pay him accordingly.

Fed up with being treated unfairly, Walt Disney, along with his brother, Roy, opened their own studio and Walt started cartooning a new character, Mickey Mouse. By adding sound to the cartoon called "Steamboat Willie," Walt Disney's new character, Mickey Mouse, made a cinematic breakthrough. Then, as they say, "The Rest Is History." Over time, Walt Disney made many correct decisions that made him one of the most exceptional people on earth.

Types of Successful Entrepreneurs

There are two kinds of successful entrepreneurs; those who have people working for them and those who have money working for them. Extremely successful entrepreneurs have both.

The world's first Billionaire, J. Paul Getty famously said. "I'd rather earn 1% from the efforts of 100 people that 100% of my own efforts." As an entrepreneur, you should be willing to investigate opportunities where you, as a team leader, can make what is known as override income from the efforts of your team members.

To be successful, you need to be an optimist. According to Winston Churchill, the pessimist sees difficulty in every opportunity while the optimist sees the opportunity in every difficulty.

Also, consider how the following adage can help you become more successful: Winners never quit and quitters never win. Persistence and consistency are the hallmarks of successful people. Clearly, the more you utilize **Entrepreneurial Thinking,** the more likely you will become successful.

Choose to be a player
rather than a fan.

To be really successful, you need to be a player rather than a fan. Several years ago, I attended a motivational workshop with several inspirational speakers.

One gentleman said that he was not a fan, he was a player. In other words, he did not spend any time watching professional sports because in his opinion, that was time wasted.

Spending hours and hours watching professional sports players who are making millions of dollars cannot specifically help you improve your own life and income.

ENTREPRENEURIAL THINKING means playing in the game of life and focusing on things that will help you improve every aspect of your life. Spending more time doing things that will help you succeed rather than spending too much time watching other people play sports can continuously help you consistently succeed.

Consider the future and plan for long-term benefits.

Plant a tree that you will never get a chance to sit under. Contribute to a cause that is greater than yourself. When you think like an entrepreneur, you plan for long tern results.

Imagine if you are starting out as a farmer. First you need to clear the land and dispose of what you removed. The next step is to till the soil and plant the seeds of what you wish to harvest. Then you need to add water and fertilizer and wait.

Now, much of the work is taking place underground as the seeds start growing roots. The roots have to come first so that they can support the plant as it starts growing out of the soil. You also need to continue to water and keep the weeds out.

Finally, the plants produce a viable fruit or vegetable. Now it's time to harvest and sell the results of all of your hard work. The farmer planned for the long term rather than seeking immediate gratification. Planning for the long term is one of the strongest attributes of **Entrepreneurial Thinking**. Doing so will also ensure your success in every endeavor you choose to accomplish.

Chapter Two

Improve Your
Finances

How to make money work for you.

Make sure that you understand some critical financial concepts, such as the power of compound interest and the rule of seventy-two.

Money will double if the number of years times the interest rate equals 72. For example, $10,000 at a 7.2% interest rate for 10 years will become $20,000. Do the math.

Understand the concept of the present value of money. What would you rather have - $1,000 today or $10,000 in 10 years? It depends on the interest rate you could get on the $1,000. There are present value calculators available on the Internet. Play with them until you understand the concept.

Another key concept is understanding opportunity costs. Opportunity costs simply means that choosing to spend money on one thing eliminates the opportunity to either save the money or spend it on something else. Whenever possible, you should consistently choose to spend less and save more.

Monitor your checking account.

Banks can make mistakes. Just ask anyone whose account was hacked or they were the victim of identity theft. If you don't keep track of your accounts, it will be difficult to prove that you didn't make that $500.00 withdrawal at the ATM last Saturday night.

Or maybe you did. But you just don't remember it. This is a totally different problem which we'll address in another chapter.

Use a home computer-based checkbook system for your checking account. This way you can categorize your expenses as you go along to see where your money is going. Quicken is one of the best. This record keeping will make doing your taxes much easier.

Also, being able to track your expenses will make it easier to understand where the holes are in your spending habits. We'll see how to do this manually a little later in this chapter.

Make a spending plan.

You don't need to adhere to a restrictive budget and deny yourself any freedom, but a general spending plan will help you track where your money goes. More people get into financial trouble because they lose sight of things they really need and just buy what they want.

No one really needs the latest and greatest wall-sized entertainment and home theater system in their living room, especially if they are already having trouble making their rent or mortgage payments.

You are not what you buy. No matter how much advertisers try to convince you that your life is worthless unless you buy their product, they are just out to make money off of your weaknesses, I have never seen a hearse pulling a u-haul-it. You are not your stuff.

Keep what you value in the forefront of your thinking. Your values, not the opinions of others, should dictate your spending habits. Spend only on things that make you happy, but spend within reason and within your ability to pay for them.

The first item on your budget should always be your savings plan. The best way is to pay yourself first and make it automatic. Starting a consistent savings plan will provide you with a sense of financial security. There is nothing else quite like the feeling of having money in the bank. Even if you have debt, having cash in the bank will make you feel more in control of your finances. Cash in the bank will also give you more options when trying to start a business or engage in other entrepreneurial endeavors.

Use the following Worksheet to figure out where your money goes. Do this exercise for at least three months, Make a list of everything you spend and everywhere you spend it. Beyond the rent, utilities, and other regular expenses, you might be surprised how much money slips through your fingers. How much did you really spend at coffee shops and dollar stores.

Now take this list and review it with an attitude of trying to save your money. Decide what things you needed versus all of the things you just wanted. See how much money you could realistically place in your savings program. You don't need to remove all fun from your life, just moderate it so you will be able to have a lot more fun later in your life. Later in your life, perhaps in retirement, you will have more time to enjoy your life.

It's okay to be poor and young. You have your whole life to build wealth. It's okay to be old and rich. You have earned the right to do what you want to do when you want to do it. It's NOT okay to be old and poor. You don't want to depend of the government, or worse, expect your family to support you.

You don't want to become one of the **RIPPERS**. **R**elatives **I**n **P**eople's **P**ockets **E**roding **R**etirement **S**avings. Your children will need to plan for their own retirement, not take care of you because you failed to do so. **Entrepreneurial Thinking** demands self-reliance.

Once you track your expenses for a few months you will be able to figure out where the holes are in your spending and you can stop it. Most of the time the choice is pretty straight-forward: Buy unnecessary stuff today or have the money to do what you want to do tomorrow. You can either, max out your credit cards today and Appear to be well-off. Or you can limit your immediate gratification by not buying stuff you really could live without and actually **Be** financially well-off tomorrow.

MONTHLY EXPENSES WORKSHEET

		MONTH 1 AMOUNT	MONTH 2 AMOUNT
MONTHLY INCOME	xxxxxxxxxxxxxxxxx		
SAVINGS 10% Minimum	xxxxxxxxxxxxxxxxx		
HOUSING Under 30%	Mortgage/Rent		
	Maintenance		
UTILITIES	Electric		
	Gas		
	Water		
	Cable/satellite		
	Internet		
	Cell phone		
TAXES	Income		
	Automobile		
	Property		
INSURANCE	Home		
	Automobile		
	Health		
	Life		

AUTOMOBILE	Auto Payment		
	Fuel		
	Bus/Taxi		
FOOD	Groceries		
	Restaurants		
ENTERTAINMENT	Movies		
	Night out		
SERVICES	Medical		
	Dental		
	Hair		
	Personal care		
MISCELLANEOUS	Clothing		
	Cosmetics		
	Toiletries		
	Cleaning		
	Laundry		
	Other		
DEBT (Less than 20%)	Loans		
	Credit Card 1		
	Credit Card 2		
CHARITIES	Church		
	Other Charities		
TOTAL EXPENSES	xxxxxxxxxxxxxxxxxx		
INCOME -- EXPENSES	(Net Income)		

Always live beneath your means.

Anyone can max out their credit cards and try to show off the affluence that they have not yet achieved or can afford. Then they can go bankrupt when they lose their job or have other financial reversals. You are not this person!

You must maintain self-control and a strong sense of self-worth not to be pressured by peers and the media to spend what you do not have. When all else fails and you think you just HAVE to have the latest and greatest technological gadget, take a deep breath and remember it doesn't matter how much money you make, it only matters how much money you keep.

There is only one way that you are guaranteed to get rich. That involves planning. Most people can't inherit enough money to become wealthy. Very few people make it with their unique talents in either sports or entertainment to become very wealthy.

The only sure way to actually get rich, or at least become financially secure, is to spend less than you make and invest your savings wisely over long periods of time.

Open a savings account for emergencies.

This savings account should have enough money in it to pay your mortgage or rent and utilities for at least 6 months. To get this much money in this account, start by pretending it is a bill to pay and that you have 3 years to pay it, then divide up the amount of money you will need into 36 easy payments and pay this account first.

If you tap into this emergency account for unexpected expenses, such as an expensive car repair, you need to put it back as soon as you can. Just start making those easy payments again until the full amount is back in the account.

Once you have completed setting up your emergency account, the next step is to start saving money for your future. The next few topics explain ways for you to consider which method is the best one for you to choose.

Start an IRA or a ROTH IRA

Which should you choose? If you need to reduce your taxes, choose an IRA. Every year when you do your taxes, you can subtract your IRA contributions from your Adjusted Gross Income on Your IRS form 1040. At retirement time, you will have to pay taxes on any money you withdraw from your IRA.

If you want to be able to take money from your account at retirement time without paying taxes, then choose a ROTH IRA. You don't get a tax reduction the year you put money into your ROTH IRA. However, according to current IRS rules and regulations, when you withdraw your money at retirement time, all of the money you withdraw from your ROTH IRA will be tax free.

You should choose a traditional IRA if you think that, like most people, your income will be less during the time you withdraw your funds which will mean your tax rate will be less in the future. On the other hand, if you think that your income and therefore your tax rate in retirement will be the same or more than it is now, then you probably should choose a ROTH IRA.

Put as much money as you possibly can into your IRA as soon as you can up to the limit allowed by the IRS. After you have your emergency fund in the bank, take a similar amount that you were paying monthly and place it into your IRA if it is within the current IRS rules.

Leave your IRA funds alone until it is time to retire; make sure you can't lose any money; make sure you don't pay too many fees.

It takes self-discipline and courage to see that money sitting there in your retirement fund and not think of ways to spend it before you retire. Many people do not have the self-control to leave this money alone. You must do so. Very few people retire with too much money.

As soon as possible, contribute the maximum amount allowed into your IRA. This maximum amount depends on how you earn money. If you are self-employed, the current IRS regulations say that you can open a SEP IRA and contribute a percentage of your adjusted gross income.

If you own a small business with employees then you could open a SIMPLE IRA. Opening a SIMPLE IRA requires that you contribute to the IRAs of your employees. If you're doing extremely well with your business, giving your employees a retirement plan will help keep good employees. Check with a financial professional or your CPA to determine which is better for you.

You should also probably look up these details on the current IRS website because the IRS changes the rules fairly often.

Begin a Pre-Tax Retirement savings plan at work.

If you work for a company that has one, contribute to a pre-tax savings plan like a 401(k), a 403(b), or a 457(b). Most large companies offer participation into a 401(k). If you are working for a non-profit organization or a school system, they should be offering a 403(b).

If you are working for a governmental entity, a 457(b) pre-tax retirement savings plan should be available. Some school systems offer both a 403(b) and a 457(b). The difference between the 403(b) and the 457(b) is the accessibility of the funds. According to current IRS regulaions, IRAs, 401(k)s and 403(b)s require the person to become 59 ½ years old before they can access their funds or they will pay an additional 10% tax penalty. Persons can acccss their 457(b) funds when they leave their employer no matter what their age. The IRS currently allows you to put away much more money into your employer-sponsored plans than you can put into your IRA. Check the current IRS rules to determine how much you can save.

If your employer offers a match, contribute at least the amount up to the maximum they will match. If they do not match, then simply use this to augment your IRA contributions. 401(k)'s and similar plans often have restrictions that your IRA doesn't have.

Every time you get a raise, place this extra money into your employer-sponsored pre-tax savings plan and continue to live as you did before your raise. Once your IRA contributions have reached the maximum, increase your contributions to your employer-sponsored pre-tax plan up to the limits allowed as well.

The same cautions apply; make sure you can't lose money; make sure you don't pay too many fees. Keep your funds for retirement. Again, almost no one retires with too much money.

Develop a disciplined savings attitude.

Remember, it doesn't matter how much money you make. It only matters how much money you keep! Also, remember to pay yourself first and make it automatic. You should always save at least 10% of your income for your financial future This savings suggestion has been around for many generations.

Don't wait until you're out of debt to start saving. Start saving as soon as you start earning money.

You have probably seen the news reports about how many lottery winners went broke within a few years of winning many millions of dollars. You wondered how anyone could be so stupid to throw away such riches. After all, you thought, with a little planning these people would have been set for life. Obviously, they wasted their money on the immediate gratification of buying frivolous, unnecessary things.

Whether or not we win the lottery, the same thing holds true for each of us. We all frequently tend to waste money on the immediate gratification of buying frivolous, unnecessary things rather than follow a consistent plan by saving money for our financial future.

Do we really need to spend $6 to $10 for a cup of coffee at a Coffee Shop every day? Fifty weeks a year of brewing coffee at home could help you put $1500 to $2500 into your savings programs. What other holes are in your daily expenditures? Use the worksheet earlier in the chapter to figure it out.

Establish credit as soon as you can.

You are only as credit worthy as the credit reporting agencies say you are, so you must control the kinds of information that they collect. Subscribe to some kind of credit monitoring service so that you can keep track of your credit score.

By law, you can get your credit reports for free once a year from each of the three credit reporting agencies. Currently, the Credit reporting agencies are Experian, Equifax, and Transunion. Contrary to popular opinion, these are NOT government agencies. They are simply multi-billion-dollar companies who earn vast amounts of money by collecting and selling your personal financial information.

These companies get paid when creditors send them information and they get paid when someone checks your credit. They do not get paid to consistently verify the accuracy of the information that they collect.

According to research, in 2019, more than 80% of the credit reports that these companies sell contain errors. It is your responsibility to review your credit reports and correct the errors.

Another tenant of **Entrepreneurial Thinking** is to keep any records of your credit worthiness correct so that if you need good credit to proceed with a money-making project it will be there when you need it.

Be careful when using a credit card.

Never use your credit card for splurge purchases and always pay every charge card off every month. Credit card fees and interest charges can really add up.

You could have bought an exercise machine on sale and placed the large amount on a high interest credit card. Unfortunately, you may have purchased a very expensive clothes hanger in your bedroom. Because of the time it takes to pay off the credit card and the interest, you could have ended up paying twice as much as the original retail price of the exercise machine.

One way to control your spending urges is to recognize your triggers. Are you someone who believes that "When the going gets tough, the tough go shopping"??? Many people get satisfaction from buying stuff and almost use spending money as therapy.

Do "HUGE SALE" advertisements catch your eye? Ok, you know you don't really need 20 boxes of your favorite cracker because they will probably go stale before you eat all of them, but it's BOGO!!

Once you can identify what behaviors trigger your unnecessary spending try to avoid the situations. Consider using cash most of the time for spending that you can't deduct on your taxes.

Use credit cards to help you track expenses. To really use credit cards to their best advantage, use different credit cards for different types of expenses.

For example, use one credit card for all of your business purchases. If you have more than one business, use a different card for each business. Use a different card for medical expenses if you have any.

Add these credit card accounts into your computer-based checkbook program and categorize all of your expenses. Use the same categories you used for your checkbook expenses and it will make doing your taxes much easier.

If you haven't been careful up to now, then here's how to get out of credit card debt.

The first thing to do is to contact every credit card company you have and ask them to increase your limit. If your credit card balance is less than 30% of your credit card limit, it will increase your credit score. Once you have increased your credit score, ask the credit card companies to lower your interest rate. You may be surprised that many credit card companies have different rates of interest. You may be able to get a lesser interest rate.

Script for Decreasing Credit Card Interest Rates

First: Call your Credit Card company

Press "0" or say "Representative" as many times as necessary to get to speak to a person.

When you finally speak to a person they will ask for your card number even if you already gave it to the phone system several times already. Be sure to write their name down – ask them to spell it.

Credit Card Company: How may I help you?

You: What is my current interest rate?

Them: They will probably give you a rate between 12% and 24%

You: I would like that interest rate lowered.

Them: Either they will say okay or they will not. If not, then proceed.

You: I'm confused. I received an offer in the mail from a different credit card company for a 0% interest rate for the next year if I transfer my funds to them. I realize that that is an introductory rate, but I am considering switching. In order for me to feel comfortable continuing to use this card as my primary card, I would think that you could be a little more competitive. Is there any way you can reconsider lowering my interest rate, at least temporarily?

Them: Either they will say yes or they will not. If not, then keep on going.

You: Thank you for your help. May I please speak to a supervisor?

When a Supervisor gets on the line:

You: Hello, I have been speaking with (the name you wrote down), but I need some additional assistance. (start over asking for a lower rate.)

Now, make a list of all of your debts; credit cards, student loans, car loan, home mortgage, and every other debt you have. Put them in a list by the interest you are being charged, highest to lowest.

If you normally pay more than the minimum payment on everything; stop it. Pay only the minimum on all of the debt with the lower interest rates. Take the extra money you were paying to all of the debts and pay it all to the one debt that has the highest interest rate.

Once this highest debt is paid off take it off the list. If it is a credit card, you may want to cancel the account and not use it again. Move the next highest interest rate debt to the top of the list and do it again. Keep repeating until all of your debt is paid off, except maybe your mortgage.

Getting your debt paid down and then paid off should allow you to increase your savings. It should not be an excuse to get deep into debt again by buying something that you don't really need.

Entrepreneurial Thinking suggests that you have goals for everything you are trying to accomplish. Make getting out of debt a major goal. These methods are the action steps you can use to achieve this goal.

Here's an example of how your list should look

Who You Owe	How Much	Interest Rate
Credit Card 1	$8,000	18%
Credit Card 2	$3,000	14%
Student Loan	$12,000	10%
Mortgage	$95,000	6%
Auto Loan	$9,000	4%

In this scenario, make only the minimum payment on everything except the credit card that you are paying 18% interest on. Pay as much as you can to pay this debt off first. Once that credit card is paid off, you probably should cancel your account. Then, delete it from the list and pay as much as possible on the 14% debt, which will now be at the top of the list.

Once you have removed the highest interest debt, rejoice in the milestone. Pat yourself on the back and buy yourself a reasonable treat. Don't get carried away. Review what you did to make it work and share your success with others who care.

Paying off the highest interest debt first and moving down the list has been called the "Snowball effect." This means as the snowball rolls down a snow-covered hill, it becomes larger as it approaches the bottom. Similarly, as your debt becomes less, as you approach the bottom of your list, your financial security becomes larger and larger.

Some advisors say you should pay off the smallest balance first. There is a psychological advantage to doing so, but that will cost you a lot more money.

Other gurus say that you should completely pay off all of your debt before you start saving any money. However, if you pay yourself first, even if you have debt, you will start a disciplined savings habit that will benefit you in the long run.

In other words, start saving money as soon as you get a job. Place at least 10% of your pay into a savings program and keep it there. Even if you have debt, pay yourself first because it is very important to pay yourself to help you have a secure financial future. Clearly, in the long run, you are the most important person to pay for your future.

Don't ever loan money to anyone.

Shakespeare got it right. "Neither a borrower nor a lender be. For loan oft loses both itself and friend. And borrower dulls the edge of husbandry." If a friend asks for a loan and you can afford it, make it a gift.

If not, then simply explain that you'd love to, but you really can't afford it. If that causes a rift in the friendship, then it wasn't much of a friendship in the first place.

Loans to family members are worse. It's hard for Cousin Ernie to look you in the eye when he knows he owes you $10,000.00 and has no intention to pay it back. Many family rifts occur over borrowed monies. Since one of the tenants of **Entrepreneurial Thinking** is being in control of your finances, you must realize that money you loan to other people is money out of your control.

Another aspect of taking financial responsibility for someone else is to cosign or guaranty. Never cosign or guaranty an obligation for someone else. If that person doesn't pay, you will be responsible for repayment.

Since you should neither a borrower nor a lender be, don't try to borrow money from friends or relatives either. You don't want to cause a rift in your relationships because of your financial problems.

Besides, if you consistently **Think like an Entrepreneur**, you will accept the responsibility for your own financial status. As such, borrowing money from friends or relatives should never be considered as an option for you to even think about.

Establish a good working relationship with a bank.

If you have a savings and/or a checking account at a bank, apply for a credit card through that bank. Ask for a relatively low credit limit such as an amount you could reasonably pay off every month.

Use it for minimal purchases that you would normally use cash or your debit card, such as gasoline or groceries.

Typically, having a credit card is more secure than having a debit card. Statistically, more people's bank accounts are negatively altered by illegal transactions and identity theft from their debit card number than their credit card number.

It is not necessary to have a $20,000 credit limit if you spend $300.00 on gasoline or groceries during the month and pay it off every month. Also, if you have established an emergency fund, then you will not need a high limit credit card for unexpected expenses.

Get Cash Back from your credit cards.

Go for the credit card that has the most cash back options. Reward points typically encourage you to purchase things you really don't need just to be able to use the reward points. Cash back options can reduce your next month's payment or allow you to add to your savings plans.

The only exception to only getting cash back is if you can use the reward points to purchase discounted gift cards at stores you normally shop at anyway.

Be Credit Smart.

If at all possible, you should save up for any major purchases; however, sometimes you have to balance the necessity of the item, like a car that you must have to get to work, with the need for credit. Be sure to shop for the money as carefully as you shop for the car.

Making this major required purchase would be a great time to contact the bank you have developed a relationship with. You may be able to negotiate a better price on your needed item like this car if you already have the financing arranged to purchase it.

Be financially independent of your parents by age 21. If you are going to graduate school for a degree that will lead to significant income opportunities you can drag it out to 25.

Financial Independence may mean working minimum wage jobs and living in a cheap apartment with a roommate who is messier than you.

Do not be one of the **KIPPERS**. **K**ids **In** **P**arent's **P**ockets **E**roding **R**etirement **S**avings are **KIPPERS**. It doesn't matter what kind of financial problem you have. After you're 25, never, ever, move back into your parent's home. You are an adult and as such, you are responsible for yourself. If you borrow money from your parents, pay them back as soon as possible.

Do not move into your parent's rental property and not pay rent and/or utilities. This is even worse than moving into their home because now you are not only causing them expenses, but you are reducing their income. Often, this arrangement can cause resentment by both parties.

If you truly think like an Entrepreneur, this scenario is probably frightening. After all, **Entrepreneurial Thinking** is being self-reliant and self-confident. You can't be either of these if you are dependent on your parents into your late 20s or 30s. It is especially frightening to the parents of **KIPPERS** who see their retirement being pushed years into the future because their adult child refuses to become self-sufficient.

Financial independence is especially critical if you have children. If your children see you as not living up to your responsibilities, you are teaching them that it is acceptable to be both lax and irresponsible. Children copy their parents.

Once your children go into the real world and compares you poorly to other parents, you will probably lose their respect, which you may never regain.

Children are much more aware than parents think they are. They will remember being hurt, frightened, or lied to for the rest of their lives and may despise you for it.

People who are always asking relatives to help them out financially are called **RIPPERS**. **R**elatives **I**n **P**eople's **P**ockets **E**roding **R**etirement **S**avings. Why should Great Aunt Edith give you money because you made some stupid mistake and can't pay your own bills? Even worse, why should you give your nephew money because he is irresponsible?

Never become a **KIPPER** or a **RIPPER** and don't allow others to make you feel like you need to support them. It may be difficult to tell your adult child "**NO**" when they ask for money because of whatever excuse they can come up with, but you must do it for their sake as well as your own.

If you continue to financially support any relative, whether they are your adult child or some other adult relative, you reinforce a sense of entitlement and dependence that the dependent adult will carry for years.

By robbing them of the consequences of their bad choices, they will fail to develop a sense of responsibility for their actions. Also, they will probably fail to develop the initiative needed to prevent their financial difficulty in the future.

You should utilize your **Entrepreneurial Mindset** to explain to the dependent adult you are trying to help them understand how they should behave. By doing so, you will be encouraging them to think like an entrepreneur and be self-reliant and self-confident themselves. This will help them improve their lives.

Invest in yourself.

Money you spend on education is not an expense; it is an investment. As with any investment, if the return on the investment is greater than cost of the investment, then it will be a good investment and borrowing money is a smart thing to do with any long term investment that will pay life-long dividends. Education is one of those life time investments.

However, borrowing money to go to college with no specific career plans and employment potential may not be a good idea. Your major in 19th century French poetry may not provide employment in a career that will allow you to pay off those student loans that you used the money to party with.

Be ready to invest in a legitimate opportunity if one presents itself. Learn how to distinguish legitimate opportunities from get-rich-quick schemes. If it seems too good to be true it probably is a scam.

As someone with an **Entrepreneurial mindset**, you should be willing to invest in your entrepreneurial endeavors to the point you can expect a positive return on your investment. Be sure to do your homework before opening your wallet.

Buy your own home.

As soon as possible, take the financial steps necessary towards home ownership. There is something about waking up in the morning, walking outside, and knowing that this is your home.

In addition to the positive emotional feelings of home ownership, there are also financial benefits. Interest you pay on the mortgage can be tax deductible if you file enough itemized deductions.

If you have become an Entrepreneur and have a business, you can potentially have a home office and can deduct a portion of your home expenses. These expenses can include utilities, insurance, computer, phone and home repairs, among others. If you have more than one business, you might be able to deduct more expenses because you have more than one home office. You should check with your tax professional or read the rules yourself to make certain that what you are deducting is allowable.

If at all possible, pay your home mortgage off before you retire. This is, of course, unless you can use the equity in your home to fund an investment that can guarantee you a rate of return greater than that of the loan.

In the 1950s, Walt Disney mortgaged his home to partially fund the original Disneyland. That worked out very well. However, you probably should not tap into the equity of your home for that investment opportunity for diamond mining in Antarctica that you read about on the Internet. Something as fishy as that is probably just an Internet scam. Always use some common sense before making such a decision.

On a personal note, using home equity is what my wife and I did to make money in real estate. We got a $250,000 line of credit on our home. We used the money to build a spec house. Although, we had to pay 6% interest on the line of credit, the loan was worth it. After two years, we were able to make a $50,000 profit on the sale of the spec house and pay off the line of credit. We didn't make the millions that Walt Disney made but we made a nice profit and put some extra money in the bank.

Do your own taxes.

Get a tax preparation software program and use it to help you organize the information that the IRS expects to find in your return. Turbo Tax is a good choice. It will walk you through filling out your tax return, but you must have the information available to fill in the blanks. If you have spent the time necessary to categorize your expenses throughout the year, you can easily plug in the information in the needed categories. You can simply use your checkbook and charge card printouts for those tax return details that you have categorized.

The more you work on your own business of the family, the more you will understand how to track your income and control your expenses. You need to realize that every family is a business in itself since running a household involves funds and expenses. Not every family engages in Entrepreneurial activities to manage money for the household. However, just like any business, every family has income and expenses and needs to manage their finances in order to improve their financial future.

As long as the IRS will let you, file a paper copy, rather than file electronically. According to some tax experts, paper copies reduce the likelihood of an audit. Either way, let the IRS deposit your refund money into your bank account. Doing this will avoid the possibility of someone stealing your IRS refund check from your mailbox.

Getting a refund on your taxes might make you feel like you are getting a bonus. Actually, you are just getting money that you let the government use for free. A smarter way to save money is to figure out how to never get a refund and never pay additional taxes when you file your tax return by the IRS deadline date.

If you are working for a company that withholds taxes, you can adjust your withholding so that you don't get a refund. This should increase your bring home amount of your paycheck every pay period. Now you need to be very frugal with your spending and put this additional income into your retirement savings program.

You could also place the additional income into a regular savings account to augment your emergency fund or the account used to pay cash for that major purchase like an energy-saving refrigerator. Placing the extra funds into your retirement account will be better in the long run and will earn you interest.

Never cheat on your taxes.

Cindy, the Collie may have cost you $5,000.00 in Vet bills this year, but you still can't deduct her as a dependent. Check what's deductible in your tax preparation program to verify what you can and cannot deduct.

Besides it was income tax evasion that eventually brought down the famous outlaw, Al Capone, not murder and racketeering. Other famous people who were targeted by the IRS include Lil' Wayne, Nicolas Cage, Willie Nelson, Wesley Snipes, and Martha Stewart. Failing to file or pay taxes can have tough consequences.

However, you need to be aware that if you receive any phone calls from anyone claiming to be from the IRS, it's a scam. Scammers use scare tactics and threaten people with immediate jail time if they don't give them a credit card or other electronic payment. Another scam is the telephone call telling you that IRS refunds are yours, but you will need to give the scammers your bank account number in order to receive the money.

The IRS only sends actual letters on official IRS letterhead and require you to respond, in kind, by mail, with information that they ask for. Don't let yourself be the victim of a scam.

How much monthly income will you need to maintain your lifestyle in retirement?

No matter how long before you actually retire, you will need to understand how much monthly income you will need once you stop working. You can use the monthly expense worksheet, recommended below, to complete the list of necessary expenses. However, depending on how long before you are planning on retiring, you might need to include the number of years of inflation to re-calculate the amounts for the year you are planning to stop working.

For example, for most of the last 30 years or so the average annual inflation rate was nearly 4% per year. The way you can calculate is as follows: for every $100.00 of today's expenses that you have listed on your monthly expense worksheet, you can expect it to cost approximately $148.00 in 10 years. If it will be 20 years until you decide to retire, the same $100.00 that you have listed on your monthly expense worksheet will cost approximately $219.00

This means that your retirement income that you will need in order to maintain your lifestyle in retirement will probably need to be much more than today's income.

You can use this list as an expectation of how much your expenses in retirement will become:

Housing and Utilities _____

Taxes and Insurance _____

Food and Entertainment _____

Auto and Transportation _____

Medical /Dental Othe _____

Miscellaneous and Debt _____

Charity and Other _____

Total income needed _____

How much monthly income will you have in retirement?

Next, you can use the following list to calculate approximately how much monthly income you believe you will have at the time that you decide to stop working. You can use this list to figure out what else you can do financially to make the total income become the total amount of funds that you expect to need at that time in your life.

Social Security _____

Company Pension _____

IRA Income _____

ROTH IRA Income _____

401k 403b 457b Income _____

Second Career _____

Total income available _____

Chapter Three

How to Make Money in Real Estate

It would be incomplete to publish a book about **Entrepreneurial Thinking** without a section on How to Make Money in Real Estate.

Real Estate is still one of the best ways to develop the entrepreneurial skills necessary to make money with your entrepreneurial thinking. Remember, it takes both a mindset and a skillset to become a successful entrepreneur. Profitable Real Estate investing can be accomplished on a part-time basis while you maintain your regular job.

When I started making money in real estate, I kept my job as a computer programmer for many years. I used my income to invest in property which I then was able to sell for a profit. I was able to borrow money to invest because I had a good income and I had good credit.

My single most profitable transaction was when I purchased a four-plex apartment as rental income for $290,000. It was actually two side-by-side duplexes.

I put some sweat-equity into the project by painting, refinishing the floors, repairing the roof and some other cosmetic touches to make the apartments more attractive to renters. FYI: Sweat Equity means doing the work yourself that increases the value of the property.

I only kept the apartments for around 6 years. Like any rental property there were many issues which reduced its profitability. Some tenants wouldn't pay on time so I had to evict them. Other tenants simply left when it was time to pay the rent so I had to clean out the apartments and have the locks changed.

Being a landlord can be challenging. The most challenging task was to be able to make the mortgage payment every month when the property was not rented every month.

Advertising to find renters takes time and money. Checking the renter's credit and preparing the rental contract also costs time and money. Keeping the property well prepared for someone else to move into it is also something that has to be done. Also, when the tenant calls because something has broken, you have to either do the maintenance yourself or pay someone else to do so.

In order to reduce my personal responsibilities on a day-to-day basis, since I had another full-time job, I contracted with a real estate company that had a rental property management department. It cost me 10% of the monthly income for them to do the advertising, credit checking, and scheduling the maintenance but it was worth it.

The profitability came when I put them on the market. I had really improved their looks, so I was able to sell them fairly quickly. I sold one of the duplexes for $219,000. That price was not bad for a $145,000 investment in only 5 years. But, the next year, I had an investor who saw a greater potential in the property and purchased the other duplex for $360,000.

The bottom line was that I purchased the property for $290,000, did some modifications and cosmetic repairs and sold it for a total of $579,000. That gave me an overall profit of $289,000, almost doubling my money. I did this while keeping my job as a computer programmer.

So let's look at some options of several ways to make money in real estate on either a part-time or full-time basis.

Wholesaling

By definition, wholesaling is buying something wholesale and selling it retail to make a profit. In real estate, the definition of Wholesaling is controlling an asset without actually buying it, yet still being able to sell it.

It is a three step process.

Step 1: Find a property that the sellers are very motivated to sell.

Step 2: Get them to agree to sell you the property for a fairly low price and to sign a contract that can be assigned to someone else.

Step 3: Sell the contract to someone else for more money than you agreed to buy the property for.

This is a fairly simple process, but doing it is not easy. There are multiple ways to find a property with motivated sellers. You can simply drive around areas and look for properties that look abandoned and contact the current owner. You can go on the county website and look up who the owner of the property is. Most of the time, you can look up the property by address. Sometimes, these delapidated properties were inherited by someone who lives in a different city and state. The new owners of the inherited properties may have no interest in that property and are more than willing to get some money for it.

You can look for properties that have signs that read "For sale by owner" and negotiate for the property. Also, you can read the obituaries and contact the family after a relatively short but respectful time. The family of the deceased may want to sell the property or work with you to sell it.

Other methods you can use are to place "bandit signs" out in neighborhoods advertising that you will "Buy Your House – Cash – Quick Closing." Of course, you are simply trying to get the property under contract so that you can sell the contract to someone else for a profit.

You could develop a website where people can give you their information about property they are trying to sell. Then you will need to advertise the website on internet advertising systems such as Craigs List or others. Some people who set up a website start with what is called a Splash Page. The Splash Page typically encourages people who view it to provide requested information more quickly than simply a home page.

Ideally, as you continue the process of wholesaling, you should build a buyers and sellers list. Doing so will help you to be able to move from one transaction to another in a relatively short period of time.

These are the basic concepts of Real Estate Wholesaling. There are many sources that are available to you for details of the methodologies to make the process work. Like any entrepreneurial endeavor, the results will be directly proportional to the amount of resources you invest.

Resources of time and money will be required in order to be successful. Wholesalers typically don't make a great deal of money on each transaction. Five thousand to fifteen thousand dollars profit per transaction is what you should expect. After all, you really haven't done anything to improve the property to increase it's value.

You have simply made money by researching and implementing the knowledge by knowing more about the value of the property than the person who signed the original contract. After you successfully develop a wholesaling business, you might want to transition into what many people consider the next step in real estate investing: Fix and Flip.

Fix and Flip

Just as it sounds, Fix and Flip means buying a piece of property, fixing it up, and selling it for a profit. Many times, a wholesaler will be selling to another real estate investor who will be actually taking a piece of property in need of repair, fixing it up, and then selling the renovated property for a profit.

Fixing and flipping is the next step in many real estate investors' business plan. First you develop the skills of finding properties that need some repairs. After the property has been fixed up and resold, you have a better chance of making a higher profit than you can with wholesaling. You can still do "fix and flip" on a part-time basis. If you cannot do the repairs yourself, you need to find contractors who will be willing to work with you to complete the renovation. If you do hire contractors, make sure that they will do what they say they will do on time and within your budget.

You can look at any of the several "fix and flip" reality shows in order to get a general idea of how the process works, Remember, however, reality TV should be called TV made Reality. Yes, they are filming people in situations that seem real, but some shows are just that – shows. They show enough to keep you interested but edit out the mishaps and actual time required to do the physical work.

Remember these are simply filmed shows. Nearly every reality show has directors and producers suggesting dialogue and close up shots to make the people in front of the cameras, often actors, talk or act in cerain ways in order to get the best coverage for the TV show.

In real life, there are no "re-does" or time compression. You cannot edit out your own errors.

You can also do research on the internet. Be aware that you can find many real-estate furus willing to sell you any number of real-estate investing systems that can cost hundreds to thousands of dollars. One lecture and one book mau not help you reach your goal.

Most of the information you find on the internet about how to do "fix and flips" are thinly disguised advertisements for one of the dozens of systems they want you to buy. While some information on the internet can give you a few ideas to get you started, they may not help you throughout the process.

None of the above methods, television or the internet will give you a complete insight into the details of actually doing a project yourself.

Here is a summary on how to do a "fix and flip:"

Step 1: Find a property that needs repair that the sellers are very motivated to sell,

Step 2: Do your research to find out how much the property should sell for if it was in better condition as with an updated kitchen and bath. This is called either Fair Market Value (FMV) or After Repair Value (ARV).

Step 3: Find a contractor willing to give you a bid for the required repairs and updates. This is called Cost of Repairs or COR.

Step 4: Make an offer on the house based on the ARV, minus the COR and minus the amount of profit you intend to make on this investment.
For example:
ARV:$200,000
COR:- $50,000
Profit: - $50,000
Offer:$100,000

Another way to do a Fix and Flip is to buy a house that has some repair issues but can be lived in right now. You can fix it up a little at a time while you live in it for a few months or years. Then, sell it for a profit of as much as you can get out of it.

After you sell it, buy another house and do it again. This is a very part-time way to accomplish a fix and flip, but some people find that it works for them.

Three Exit Strategies

With either wholesaling or Fix and Flip as a goal, the first step is finding a property with motivated sellers that are willing to sell their property for less than the current fair market value (FMV).

Finding a motivated seller is the first step. It does not matter what the motivation is. The property may require quite a bit of repair; the seller needs the funds; the property is an unwanted inheritance. or any other reason. Finding that motivated seller is the key to success.

1. Wholesaling is the first exit strategy. You acquire the property ownership rights with a contract of sale that allows you to sell the contract for a profit by assigning the contract to someone else. Having done so, you will have successfully completed the Wholesaling strategy.

2. With Fix and Flip, you can simply sell the property once you have performed all of the required property improvements so that you can sell it for a profit.

3. Another option, is the "Cash Flow" option. You acquire the property and have taken whatever steps that were necessary for the property to be ready for occupancy. Then you can simply turn the property in rental property to create a positive cash flow.

The "cash flow" option sets the stage for you to potentially generate a steady stream of income month after month and year after year. Actually, consistent "Cash Flow" is the ultimate goal.

As a successful entrepreneur, you want to be earning money with passive income. By definition, "Passive Income" means income that you don't have to work at earning every day. Rental Income is the most utilized type of passive income.

Tax Sales

Every month, most municipalities sell property, which have unpaid delinquent taxes, on the courthouse steps. Depending on what state you are in, you can potentially buy the property for only the amount of the delinquent taxes.

Before you participate in showing up at the courthouse on Tax Sale day, make certain that you understand the rules of the state you are going to work in. Every state has a set of rules that investors participating in acquiring property via a Tax Sale need to understand before they try to succeed in making a profit.

Some states allow investors to bid much more than the taxes that are owed. It might still be a good investment because as the investor, you can sometimes earn 20% or more on the total amount you pay for the property. In other words, if the original property owner reclaims the property, they will have to pay you 20% more than you paid the municipality at the tax sale. This 20% profit on tax sales is currently available in the state of Georgia. You will need to determine how the tax sales work in your state.

If the original owners don't reclaim the property that you have paid the taxes on, then you will have purchased the property for the total amount you paid the municipality. Just be careful not to overpay for the property. Do your due diligence before tax sale day in order to make sure you make a profit whether the previous owner reclaims the property or you take ownership of it.

Due Diligence is critical in order to make sure that what you pay for the property will ensure your ability to make a profit. By definition, Due Diligence in tax sale real estate essentially means verifying the exact address of the property and the amount of recent sales prices of nearby similar properties.

I live in Georgia, and I have made quite a bit of money acquiring property offered by both city and county selling property for delinquent taxes. When the existing owner reclaimed their property, I made an immediate 20% return on my investment. To get the profit, I have to provide them a quitclaim deed that says I have relinquished my right to claim the property.

If the existing owner does not reclaim their property, then in Georgia, there is a legal process that you have to go through to become the official owner of the property. Once you pay the county or city, you get an indentured deed that says you are the conditional owner of the property.

The original owner has a specific period of time to redeem their property. After the time to redeem has expired, then you must go through a process to file a "Bar of Redemption" which is essentially a foreclosure on the previous owners right to redeem. This "Bar of Redemption" requires you to hire an attorney to complete the process where you become the actual owner of the property.

Foreclosure and Pre-Foreclosure Sales

Every month, mortgage companies foreclose on properties and sell them on the Courthouse steps. At this point, it is possible to purchase the property for only what is owed on it and the previous property owner will lose their equity. Again, doing your due diligence is critical to make sure that you are not paying more than the property is actually worth.

If you can find property that is going to be foreclosed on before it actually gets to the courthouse steps, you have the potential to make more money. This is pre-foreclosure. Many people, especially people who own commercial or rental property, might be willing to allow you to take over their payments. Sometimes, they are willing to lose their equity in order to prevent the negative credit results of being foreclosed upon.

The best way to accomplish this is a legal contract whereby the deed to the property is transferred to a new owner under the heading of "Subject To." In this scenario, the investor simply takes over the payment from the previous property owner and starts making the payments.

This way, the investor essentially also takes over the equity in the property. Now the investor can sell the property to another person and get some or all of the equity that the previous property owner used to have.

As always, however, you need to follow one of the Seven Habits of Highly Effective People and Begin with the End in Mind. You need to have a methodology to find buyers before you purchase an investment property or you might wind up having to make payments far longer than you intended. This would cause you to make much less money than you could have made if you had sold the property sooner.

Like any investment, Real Estate investing can make you a lot of money or you could lose money if you don't plan well and take the necessary steps when you need to do them.

Another major part of **Entrepreneurial Thinking** is to do what needs to be done when it needs to be done, not when you get around to it.

Chapter Four

Become More Self-Aware

Never lie to the person in the mirror.

Do not deceive yourself into believing you are someone you are not. There is an old saying that goes, "You can fool some of the people all of the time and all of the people some of the time, but you cannot fool all of the people all of the time." However, you should never mislead yourself at any time. Only if you accept who you are, can you take the steps necessary to improve yourself.

You may occasionally lie to someone else if you do so with a generous spirit. "No, that dress looks great on you, Baby; your butt looks fine!"

Still, you should never lie to the person who looks back at you from your reflection. Constant self-delusion is a trap and can spiral into a life lost.

In the Disney movie Aladdin, Aladdin was talking to the Genie who had turned himself into a Bee. Aladdin asked the Genie, "How should I act when I meet the Princess?" The Genie said "BEEEEE Yourself."

Besides, who else could you be? Everyone else is already taken. Better to be a first-rate version of you than a second-rate version of someone else. Try to understand that the person in the mirror is the concept artist, the designer, and the construction crew that is creating your life every day. While you're looking into that mirror, you need to like what you see. Don't focus on imperfections that other people might not even notice. Once in a while do the naked mirror exercise where you stand naked in front of the mirror and learn to appreciate your body.

Look at yourself. Appreciate that your skin is doing a good job holding all of your internal organs where they belong. Your stomach is doing a great job processing the food you eat into energy that allows you to do all the tasks of living. Your ears help you hear beautiful music as well as the sounds of your partner telling you that you are loved. Your eyes can see beautiful landscapes and flowers as well as the magnificent sunset. You get the idea.

For best results, talk out loud to your various body parts. Hearing your own voice will reinforce your thoughts and make it less likely that you will focus on imperfections. Just do it when no one else is around to hear what is going on. Hearing you proclaim your affection for any specific body part could be concerning for anyone listening outside the door of your bathroom. You don't want anyone to call the local mental health authorities

According to Linda Creed, in the song by the same name, "The Greatest Love of all" is learning to love yourself. It's always okay to be who you are. Just don't lose sight of who you have the potential to become. Lucille Ball said "You really have to love yourself to get anything done in this world."

Always strive to be a better person than you are.

Every day is a new opportunity to take that first step towards becoming a superior you and for you to decide who you are destined to become.

We grow because we struggle to achieve and overcome obstacles. Focus on your abilities and your potential. Especially, on what you can do rather than what you can't do. By focusing on what you can do, you begin the process of using existing skills, knowledge, and abilities as a foundation for making progress in any new endeavor you choose to attempt

At any given moment, if you are unsure of how you are doing, ask yourself if you are doing your best. If the answer is "no," then figure out what is holding you back. Then, make corrections to your attitude or your efforts and do better.

Entrepreneurial Thinking requires you to always do the best you can do every day and for everything you do. Always do the right thing at the right time for the right reason.

Believe it and you can achieve it.

This is the foundation of the belief system that will allow you to accomplish any goal that you set for yourself. If you believe in yourself and believe that you can accomplish any specific thing, then you probably can do it if you understand the steps to accomplish your goal.

The only place where your dream becomes impossible is in your own mind. Only you can stop you from fulfilling your hopeful and realistic dreams.

Most of the time, you are only being held back by your own fear and insecurity. **FEAR** is only **F**alse **E**xpectations **A**ppearing **R**eal. According to Marie Curie, nothing in life, is to be feared, it is only to be understood.

According to Winston Churchill, "Courage is rightly esteemed the first of human qualities because it has been said it is the quality which guarantees all others."

Dreaming is a form of planning and your lucky day is the day you decide to "Get It Done." This would be the day you decide to begin to take the action steps necessary to move your desired outcome from the realm of your imagination into reality.

If you don't try at all, you will fail 100% of the time. **Thinking like an Entrepreneur** means that theoretically, for all things you want to accomplish, you need to essentially step up to the plate and swing for the bleachers.

Give everything you are trying to accomplish your best shot. You might be surprised at how often you will succeed.

Be independent of both the criticisms and praises of others.

You know yourself better than anyone. Fame is fleeting and not all criticisms are justified. When you are able to accept both praise and criticism and simply say, "Thank you," you will have mastered yourself and your improved your self-image.

Saying "thank you" for praise acknowledges your appreciation for the compliment and your appreciation for the person who gave it to you. If you attempt to be humble and act as if it were nothing, then you have belittled the acclaim and the person who just praised you. If you do this often enough then you will probably begin to get fewer compliments.

We all need to feel appreciated for our accomplishments. Take the praise in the spirit it was offered and express sincere gratitude.

It will be difficult to say "thank you" for being criticized. However, you should not make excuses or assign blame for criticism. If the criticism is justified, then you must do better in the future. If it isn't, then nothing you can say will make a difference anyway.

Still, you shouldn't make excuses, or worse, try to blame someone or something else. Many times, excuses are simply tools of the incompetent. Excuses are used by the weak to build monuments to nothingness. Those who use them are fools and seldom amount to anything. **Entrepreneurial Thinking** requires you to find methodology to correct issues rather than simply make up excuses for bad decisions.

The best way to diffuse criticism is to acknowledge that the other person has a right to their opinion even if you think that they're totally mistaken. Just say something like, "Really?? What do you think would be better?" This immediately puts them on the defensive without your having to admit to any mistakes.

Listen intently. They actually might have a good idea that you could use. Ask more questions until one of two things happens. One, their answers help them to realize that your solution was correct in the first place. Or, two, you realize that their ideas have some merit and can help you improve what you were trying to accomplish or help you determine a better solution.

Entrepreneurial Thinking pretty much requires you to be flexible, You should consider all options, and choose the solution that you believe will have the best outcome. Again, always try to do the right things at the right time for the right reason.

Be aware of your mental imagery.

You are who you think you are.

If you see yourself as someone who is happy to be alive and walk around with your head held high and your shoulders held back, then that is who you will be.

If you see yourself as someone who, if it weren't for bad luck, you'd have no luck at all and walk around with your shoulder's stooped and a hang-dog expression, then that's who you will be.

Either way, others will treat you the way you treat yourself. This negativity will reduce your daily opinions of yourself and reduce your options to improve yourself.

In other words, **Entrepreneurial Thinking** requires you to always have a positive attitude and take the steps necessary to have a good opinion of yourself. By doing so, you will improve your self-image and your self-esteem.

The best way to keep a good opinion of yourself is to focus on memories of good things you have done in the past. This includes the opinions of people who care about you. Also, focus on good things you expect to do in the near future.

Keeping a list of wonderful memories that you can review frequently will definitely help you keep a good opinion of yourself and your abilities. Perhaps if you could make a list of memories like your success in a sport when you were younger. Also, you could include a successful choice you made when you were originally dating your significant other. Think about including other memories that make you feel good.

Realize that you are at once both better and worse than you think you are.

The challenge is in understanding yourself enough to realize which is which. If you are very good at something, be proud but not arrogant. If you are not good at something you want to be better at, do what it takes to become more proficient.

What if you think you are good at something but an independent judge thinks otherwise? What do you think that you are terrible at, but other people think you do okay? A lot of your opinions are based on how you perceive yourself and your abilities.

If you've ever been to a karaoke contest, you have undoubtedly heard some people whose horrible singing made you cringe. Most of these people have no idea how terrible they sound. This is an excellent example of someone thinking they are wonderful but in reality, they are awful.

At that same karaoke contest there may be listeners who resist getting up to sing because they don't believe that they are very good. Then once they take the plunge and start singing into the microphone, they aren't half-bad. In this case their perception of their ability is skewed into the negative direction.

That's why you need to be realistic in your self-assessment for all of your talents and abilities. This is what is meant in the beginning of this chapter when you were cautioned to be honest with the person you see in your reflection.

Understand that you are multiple personalities.

We are all potentially many people for many people. You are one person for your partner. You are someone else for your children. If you parents are still around, then you are someone else for them.

You are someone else for the people you work with. The relationships with people at work is different especially if you are their supervisor or if someone else is your supervisor. You probably are someone else for the people you go to church with. Primarily, you are a different person for everyone who you have different relationships with.

The key to behaving correctly in all of these different relationships is to consistently use your **Entrepreneurial Thinking** to focus on always doing the right thing at the right time for the correct reason. Doing so will enhance your relationships in all of these situations.

Use affirmations to become who and what you want to be.

Affirmations are very powerful positive mental images that you can use to improve yourself. First of all, this set of positive affirmations will help you to improve your self-image and build your self-esteem.

I am a good person. I want only the best for both myself and others in my ongoing relationships. I have an abundance of high self-esteem. I am lovable and capable. Every day, I feel better about myself. I am always sufficient enough to do everything I choose to do. I am smart enough, experienced enough, and talented enough to accomplish whatever I want to do.

Everything good in me increases and multiplies every day when I do what I do. I always take control of my life. Every day, I am free to do anything and everything I want to do if I move forward to do so. I can be successful to be the person I wanted to be. My life is positive and enjoyable.

Every Day and every way, I can become more successful if I do the right things at the right time in the right way for the right reason. I am worthy and deserving of love, wealth, and success. I clearly understand that my thoughts are creating my actual reality. I always practice to understand and improve my positive self-talk.

Consciously, my mind only holds one thought at a time so that I can focus on accomplishing each of my goals. I always have only positive thoughts to support me at every level of my existence. I only say positive things to myself so that I can dismiss negative thoughts.

Every day I increase my self-esteem in every way. I work to improve myself with every activity I accomplish. Improving myself is enjoyable. I am always attempting to learn new and better ways to do things that I want to do. I am able to do whatever I set my mind to do.

The best outcome of every event is always what I expect. I understand that I am responsible for every aspect of my life. Because I accept responsibility, it encourages other people to respect me. My life is consistently a creation of my choices and activities. I will always create my life how I want it to be.

Every day, I focus on becoming the type of person I want to be. I accept myself the way I am as long as I do so positively. I always try to be able to do the best I can by understanding the goal I am attempting to achieve. I stay at peace with myself in order to acquire all that I need.

I accept the concept that I am worthy of all things positive. I deserve that my dreams will come true as long as I do the right things at the right time for the right reason.

Believe it or not, thoughts are things. What goes on between our ears is what determines our success in every area of our lives.

The Key to the Financial Freedom we desire, the success we yearn for, and the personal fulfillment we hope for is all directly related to connecting our conscious mind to our sub-conscious mind. However, knowing it intellectually isn't the same thing as truly believing it enough to take action.

In order to take action you need to reprogram your subconscious mind. Our sub-conscious mind has no ability to judge whether or not the information being given to it is true or not. The sub-conscious mind is just a recorder. It only understands positive statements in the present-tense. It relates emotional feelings to the positive statements you give it.

Once our sub-conscious mind accepts some idea as a fact, it will change our behavior to make it become true. For example, if you weigh 200 pounds and want to lose weight down to 175 pounds, then you can write an affirmation that states, "I eat only enough healthy foods to keep my body at my healthy weight of 175 pounds."

Place this affirmation where you will read it dozens of times throughout the day. As you read it, you will begin to eat differently, and over time, you will become the weight you want to be.

You can use this method to make significant changes in any aspect of your life.

Here are some examples of bad affirmations:

- **I weigh 200 pounds** and I am going to lose 25 pounds.
- I am not going to **eat junk foods** any more.
- **I am** not going to be **poor** any more.

- **I hate my job** and I want to do something else.

Because the subconscious mind only understands positive statements in the present tense it only understands the bold print in the last four statements. It only understands:

- **I weigh 200 Pounds**
- **I eat junk foods**
- **I am poor**
- **I hate my job**

Good affirmations:

- I am happily maintaining my healthy weight of 175 pounds.
- I am enjoying the healthy foods that I am eating every day so I can maintain my healthy weight.
- I am pleased to have enough income that I can take care of my family and provide them an upscale lifestyle.
- I am glad to be a successful entrepreneur.

You might wonder whether or not these Affirmation things actually work. How could me telling myself something that I know is NOT true make me behave in a way to make them become true?

When I was in my 40s, I weighed over 220 pounds. I used affirmations to lose nearly 80 Pounds. It took me almost a year, but I changed my eating and exercise habits all because every day I read my affirmations.

I placed them by my bathroom mirror so I saw them every morning and every night. I had them taped to the visor on my car so I could read them whenever I was stopped in traffic.

I remember going to the cookie store in the mall and I bought one of those giant oatmeal cookies with icing in the middle. I took one bite of it and remembered my affirmation about only eating enough healthy foods to maintain my body's healthy weight. I threw the rest of the cookie in the trash. My affirmation changed my behavior and my goal of being a healthy weight became true.

So, how should you do your affirmations?

Write a set of affirmations on three index cards (Use your computer and print it on card stock or hand write on real index cards). Choose only a few things at a time and focus on those.

1. Place one card on your bathroom mirror or someplace where you will see it and read it first thing in the morning.

2. Place one card in your car over your visor and read it when you drive to or from work when you're stuck in traffic.

3. Place one next to your bed so you can read it the last thing before you go to sleep.

Writing, posting goals, and reading them often are the keys to success. Reading affirmations just before falling asleep is the most important time to read them, so that your mind will process them while you sleep.

So how long will this take? The critical number is 21 days. If you read your affirmations every day for a minimum of 21 days you will start to develop new habits. Once you start seeing the results you want – keep on going. It's not smoke and mirrors and there are no magic tricks

This new behavior will be difficult but it will work.

Other Affirmations that can be helpful:

- I enjoy doing aerobic and resistance training every day.
- I keep my office neat and organized.
- I organize my tasks efficiently.
- I am a good person.
- I am worthy of love and success.

Know your strengths.

Never let someone else belittle your abilities or define who you are or what you are capable of. Eleanor Roosevelt said it best when she said, "No one can make you feel inferior without your consent."

"Sticks and stones can break my bones but words will never harm me." This is a truism that you should take to heart. This is one of the tenants of **Entrepreneurial Thinking**: unshakable self-confidence. If you are secure in your knowledge of yourself you don't need to be worried whether or not others are "politically correct" when they are talking to you or about you.

You know that you are worthy of all good things in life no matter what anyone else thinks of you. Whether negative comments are racist, sexist, ageist, or any other 'ist they cannot affect you unless you give other people power over you by giving power to their words.

Don't give anyone else power over you. By allowing this action to influence you, your belief in yourself or your self-confidence could be negatively affected. Again, one of the basic tenants of **Entrepreneurial Thinking** is unshakable self-confidence.

Accept that there are bigger things to worry about.

The adage, "Don't sweat the small stuff" should be a motto for thinking like an entrepreneur. Look for solutions. Look for opportunities. Do not allow yourself to focus on unimportant events. Ask yourself, "Will this really matter in 5 years?"

Being the "bigger" person takes patience and courage. Once when I was a small child, a relative came to visit us. He gave me a dime and my older brother a nickel. My greedy older brother tried to convince me that because the nickel was larger than the dime the nickel was worth more.

I knew that the dime was worth ten cents and the nickel was only worth five cents. However, I decided that if my older brother thought it was okay to cheat his little brother, it was worth it to me to "be the bigger" person and let him take advantage of me. That way, I understood that I was letting him feel superior. I know I was the one in control.

I also understood that I was being morally correct and he was being morally wrong. Being ethical in your actions is the trait worthy of respect and will bring loyalty from your followers and business dealings. Being consistently morally correct is one of the ways that thinking like an **Entrepreneur** will make your life better in all areas of life.

Be aware of your abilities.

Measure yourself against what you can do that you have not yet done rather than compare yourself to anyone else. Take an inventory of what you can do. Do this exercise and keep the results to read whenever you are feeling overwhelmed.

Start by writing down everything you can do that you once couldn't do. When you were younger, tying your shoe, telling time, riding a bicycle, and driving a car are all things you had to learn at one time in your life. Be generous with yourself and list things that you might find silly; like being able to color inside the lines of a coloring book.

Make a list of at least 20 things you are good at. Then make another list of 10 things that you want to learn how to do. Break these into smaller tasks and you might be surprised that you already have some of the skills needed to accomplish what you want to learn.

For example: What if you want to be better at meeting people? What are the skills necessary to meet people? At the basic level, being able to speak and being able to hear is mandatory. After that you need to learn when to speak and when to listen. This is not as easy as it sounds. Remember the adage that you have two ears to listen and one mouth to talk.

Most of us are poor listeners. In order to feel comfortable meeting people we should assume that we will be liked and act accordingly. By believing that we will be liked, we will behave more naturally and come across as friendlier. Be pleasant, smile, make eye contact, offer a warm handshake, ask questions and listen intently.

Focus on Positive communication methods

A smile is understood in every language on earth. It can break the ice, but you still need to speak to people in a language they understand.

What I mean by this is that you need to talk to people without jargon, industry-speak, regional colloquialisms, or buzz-words.

When asking questions go beyond "What do you do?" Ask how do they do, what do they do and how do they like what they do. Then find a way to compliment them. Not only will they feel better about themselves but also, they'll like you for your helping them to feel good.

By encouraging them to talk about themselves you will be perceived as a great conversationalist even if you don't talk much. They will feel better about themselves and will, in turn, like you better.

Never be a one-upper who always tries to outdo the other person. If they have a dog, it isn't necessary to tell them how much better your dog is. The same is true for a child or any experience they happen to share with you. No one likes to hear someone say, "Well, I've got a better story than that."

Your goal is to understand the other person so that you can build a relationship. Some relationships can morph into a mutually beneficial business relationship. You should always "seek first to understand and then to be understood." This is the one of the seven habits of highly effective people that Stephen Covey recommends.

It's okay to share similar stories or experiences in order to build rapport. However, you should not fall into the trap of trying to prove that you are smarter, more well-read, or better than they are in any way. To do so will lose the opportunity to build what could have become a very successful relationship.

Even better, share stories where you aren't the brightest and the best. Let them know that you're human and imperfect. Tell stories on yourself where you messed up and laugh at yourself. Most successful comedians use this technique.

They won't be laughing at you, they'll be laughing with you. Not only will they like you better and want to be around you more, they will identify more with you and are more likely to want to build a long-term relationship.

As a potentially successful **Entrepreneur**, the more positive long-term relationships you engage in, the more likely you will become successful in your entrepreneurial endeavors.

Learn to recognize and embrace your talents.

Try different things: write a story, draw a picture, put together a model, or sing a song. If you find that you have a talent for something, cultivate that activity.

There is a famous story from the early 20th century about a circus coming to town. As they were getting ready for the circus parade through main street, they discovered that their trumpet player was too ill to play. The bandmaster announced to the crowd that they needed a trumpet player and one young man stepped up and volunteered. They put him in costume with the rest of the marching band, gave him a trumpet and headed trough the town with all of the circus performers and animals marching along.

When the bandmaster waved his baton and struck up the band the most horrible, screeching noises blasted out of the trumpet. The animals panicked. The horse-drawn carriages crashed as they ran off the road and general mayhem brought the parade to a humiliating halt.

During the clean-up from the chaos, the bandmaster confronted the young trumpet-player and said "I thought you claimed that you could play the trumpet." The young man replied, "I didn't know I couldn't play the trumpet, I had never tried."

So, if you're going to try to engage in a new creative endeavor, you might want to practice before you try to perform in public.

Accept your imperfections, but never your shortcomings.

Use these definitions:

Imperfections are things about yourself that you wish you could change, but you really have no control over. Examples are, "I wish I weren't so short, tall, left-handed, etc."

Shortcomings are things that you can change if you choose to spend the time and effort. You can correct things such as, "I wish I wasn't so fat, skinny, uneducated, etc."

One of the most important shortcomings that many people need to improve on is their ability to speak clearly. To determine if you need to improve your ability to speak clearly, record your voice and listen critically. Many people never listen to a recording of themselves and don't realize how shrill or raspy their voice sounds until they do this exercise.

If you voice sounds relatively unpleasant to you, it probably sounds unpleasant to others. To correct this problem, take the time to practice speaking. Pick a book you like to read or a selection from a famous speech and record yourself reading it out loud. Then listen to the recording. Do this over and over until you like the way you sound.

To speak effectively, you should vary the pitch and tone. Listen to Dr. Martin Luther King's "I have a Dream" speech. Pay attention to the way his voice rises and falls in order to emphasize certain points.

Listen to John Fitzgerald Kennedy's "We choose to go to the Moon" speech. Pay attention to the way he uses comparable vocal patterns for emphasis. Although you are not trying, necessarily, to become a world-class orator you need to use similar inflections and cadences when you are trying to persuade anyone to do anything.

If you are in sales and you have scripts that you use, record yourself reading them. It will help you memorize the key points so that when you are with a prospective client, you won't sound like you're using a memorized script, but you won't forget anything.

Understand that everyone is in sales

By the way, everyone is in sales. Robert Lewis Stevenson said "Everyone lives by selling something." Every time you ever tried to persuade anyone to do anything, you were in sales. You were in sales when you were dating and wanted another date. You were in sales when you tried to get your parents to buy you a car.

You were in sales when you were asking for that promotion at your job. You are in sales when you try to persuade your significant other to go to that restaurant that you like or go on vacation where you want to go.

You are in sales if you are in school and you are trying to persuade your classmates to vote for you as class president. You are in sales if you are in school and are trying to persuade your teacher that your answers to your last exam were actually correct and you should not have failed the test.

Everyone is in sales all of the time. Either you are trying to persuade someone else to use your product or service, or you are trying to persuade yourself to get up every day and get moving because you have things that need to be done.

Entrepreneurial Thinking is acknowledging that you are in sales all of the time. The main focus of thinking like an entrepreneur is to convince yourself that you need to be motivated every day to work on your goals to make your life better.

Never talk down to yourself.

Sure, you may not be the sharpest tool in the shed, but you're certainly not the dullest either. Accept the fact that there are always smarter people than you in the world. However, that fact has nothing to do with you trying to become consistently better.

Always engage in positive self-talk. You might even need to occasionally look in the mirror when no one else is looking at you and raise your arms in triumph. Do this even if you have nothing specifically to be triumphant about. It will still make you feel better.

Ignore your inner critic.

Your main inner critic is fear. Fear is simply **F**alse **E**xpectations **A**ppearing **R**eal. Frank Herbert was correct in the book "Dune" when he said, "Fear is the mind killer." Fear can immobilize you. The opposite of fear is courage. Have the courage to fail. Failure is just one way that what you were trying to do didn't work.

During an interview, Thomas Edison was asked how it felt to fail to make a light bulb over a thousand times. He responded that he had not failed a thousand times, in fact he had not failed even once. He said that he had succeeded in proving that over a thousand different substances would not work. He then said that once he has eliminated all of the ways that will not work, he will find the way that will work.

Winston Churchill has been credited with another quotation regarding failure. He stated that, "Success is being able to go from failure to failure without losing your enthusiasm." Clearly this ability to go from failure to failure and still be enthusiastic about his project was what kept Thomas Edison motivated in his quest to perfect the incandescent light bulb.

Imagine a different reality.

Don't get caught in a rut of always doing the same things in the same way. Try new things; expand your abilities and your horizons. Step outside of your comfort zone.

There was a famous study of the processionary caterpillar that typically follow one behind the other when they travel. A researcher placed a number of these insects on a rather large flower pot so that they were nose to tail in a continuous circle.

They walked around the edge of the pot continuously for over 8 days and they all died from starvation and exhaustion. Food was nearby. However, their instincts, habits, or whatever genetic predispositions that caused them to blindly follow each other was stronger than self-preservation.

Your habits may not make you walk around and around in a circle for days and days but you need to shake things up occasionally. Habits repeated patterns, and stagnate ways of thinking become deeply ingrained. Typically, we are comfortable with our habits whether they are good or bad. Most of us tend to think "Inside the Box" when freedom and success could be only one step away.

Get creative with your life. You may find that the new talent you discovered was the best thing that ever happened to you. In order to discover your new talent, you have to try something you haven't tried before.

Perhaps, at the very least try to do something in a way you haven't tried to do it before. Pick a task that you ordinarily do a particular way and try to think of another way to do it that might be more efficient or effective.

One caution, however, when you choose a new way to do something, you should endeavor to improve the process. Clearly, choosing to do something in a more difficult manner, just for the sake of variety, would be counter-productive.

Doing tasks in a new way that is more effective and efficient is certainly a way to reinforce the positive result of **ENTREPRENEURIAL THINKING.**

Realize that only you can make you happy.

Other people may do things that please you, but ultimately it is your responsibility to make yourself happy. Happiness doesn't come from external things, but from our general attitude towards life. If we have a great attitude towards life, then we will find that life, correspondingly, will seem happier. Find happiness in small things and be grateful.

The ultimate source of our happiness is our mental attitude. When we think happy thoughts, the happiness shows in our faces and keeps us healthier. Happier people tend to be healthier. Also, a famous saying is that "Laughter is the Best Medicine." Happiness raises you up but true joy keeps you flying high. Your happiness comes first, but it should never be at the expense of another. That isn't happiness that is exploitation.

When faced with circumstances that seem negative, always look for the silver lining in what seems to be a cloud of despair. If you get fired from your job, maybe this is the time to look for an entrepreneurial opportunity.

According to Disney history, Walt Disney was fired from his first animation job at the Kansas City Star newspaper because his editor felt he lacked imagination and had no good ideas. Walt Disney believed so strongly in himself and his own abilities that he eventually decided to open his own cartoon studio.

Luckily, his brother, Roy Disney, understood finances and believed in Walt's talent as well. The two of them started the Disney Studios. The rest, as they say, is History. Disney found his silver lining. Your silver lining is waiting for you.

Accept the simple fact that some days you are the windshield and some days you are the bug.

Don't take it personally. The windshield did not set out that day to destroy the bug and the bug certainly did not intend to kill itself for the sole purpose of making the windshield difficult to see out of.

Most of the time, however, the Universe is simply not particularly interested in any specific windshield or bug.

You have to do what you can with what you have and where you are. The adage of "Bloom where you are planted" is a good beginning for accepting who you are but not of what you can be. Acceptance of negative consequences is the first step in overcoming them.

Once you find out what you did to achieve a negative result, you can learn how to avoid it the next time. Just make sure you take good notes so you won't make the same mistake twice.

ENTREPRENEURIAL THINKING means making sure you clearly accept your responsibility to do everything you can do in the best manner possible.

Embrace your mistakes.

Use your mistakes as a learning tool and grow from them. This way you can learn true humility. Besides, if you're not making mistakes, then you're not making decisions.

When faced with any decision, just decide. When uncertain about which course of action you should follow, choose one. Even a less than perfect choice is better than the immobility of indecision.

Indecision is a trap. Indecision is the first cousin to procrastination. Procrastination is stagnation. You can't accomplish anything if you can't get out of your own way.

Don't over-analyze. It's easy to fall into the snare of analysis paralysis. Every day we come to the best conclusions we can, given the information we have at the time.

Make a decision and move forward. If the decision turns out to be less productive than you wanted it to be, simply modify the decision when faced with similar circumstances next time.

Accept your humanity but never your prejudices.

We have all been programmed with who we are, who the "right kind of people" are, for us, and how we should react to any others who are different. One of the most difficult tasks we will have is overcoming our childhood brainwashing by well-meaning caregivers who simply taught us what they had been taught when they were children. Sometimes our caregivers really did not understand that what they were passing negative responses to the next generation.

There is a scene in the first Harry Potter book where Draco Malfoy tries to persuade Harry that Ron Weasley and Hermione Grainger weren't acceptable people to associate with. Harry immediately recognized Malfoy's haughtiness and prejudices and rightly surmised that Malfoy was correct in that some people should be excluded from one's association.

Malfoy, just didn't care that his own arrogance and bigotry made him the type of person that Harry Potter should exclude from his personal circle of friends. Remember the saying "Lie down with dogs, get up with fleas." Choose your close associates wisely.

Each of us needs to recognize that not everything we learned about people from other ethnic and economic backgrounds is true. We need to assess behavior on an individual basis rather than assume that we know how a particular person will behave in a certain situation based on their ethnicity or gender. Stereotyping or profiling is degrading and dangerous. **Thinking like an entrepreneur** means to rise above such prejudices.

Stereotypes, however, of any specific ethnic or economic group do exist. Mostly, they exist in movies and television where writers exploit particular groups to make a profit. However, many people do behave similarly in similar groups. Business people behave like business people, teachers behave like teachers, store clerks behave like store clerks, criminals behave like criminals, and so forth.

Martin Luther King said that people should only be judged by the content of their Character. You should allow people's individual behavior to determine your interaction with them.

Never make assumptions about any individual based upon stereotypes. Individuals have the right to act appropriately for whatever endeavor they are engaged in. Be ethical and self-reliant in judgements.

As a person with an **Entrepreneurial mindset**, you understand that you should judge people for their appropriate actions on an individual basis. If they act inappropriately, then you understand that you should judge them for their inappropriate actions on an individual basis.

Be the change you want to see in the world.

Never forget that you have the power to change the world, even if it is only in your own special corner of the world.

Stand up for a cause you believe in. Join a group to support a positive cause. Write a letter to the editor of your local paper to address something you think should be done differently. Attend and speak out at community meetings.

You may not see an immediate change in what you are trying to accomplish, but little actions can have dramatic results in the long run. You never know what kinds of future events will be triggered by your actions today!

Throwing a pebble into a lake can cause ripples on a distant shore. If one pebble isn't enough try throwing a larger stone. Be careful though. If you throw a rock large enough to cause a tsunami on the opposite shore, the backsplash could also drown you.

According to some meteorologists, there is a possibility that a small wind current can have dramatic effects on the weather. This is called the butterfly effect. Allegedly, there is a possibility that if a butterfly flaps its wings in a particular location, the rippling effect could cause a horrific massive wind storm somewhere in the distance. This is another example of how small efforts can have large results.

In the Serenity Prayer, people ask God to first, give them serenity to accept the things they cannot change. Then for God to give them the courage to change the things they can and finally, to have the wisdom to know the difference.

You might consider a rewrite of the Serenity Prayer:

God, Grant me The Courage to TRY to change the things I believe I can change;

The Wisdom to know when I should stop trying to change something because for whatever reason, it is obviously something beyond my ability to positively change it;

And then, give me the Serenity to accept the things I could not change, and the intelligence to understand why I was unable to change what I wanted to change. Allow me to stop worrying about things that are out of my control. But first give me the Courage to TRY.

One of the best ways to focus on **ENTREPRENEURIAL THINKING** is not only to work on improving he way you do everything you do, but also, to work on how to make the world a better place for you and everyone you care for.

Practice trying to be quiet for your self-analysis.

A moment of quiet is refreshing as well as peaceful for the thought process. If you can't sit and think quietly for 15 minutes or so without falling asleep or checking on your smart phone, it doesn't count.

You can meditate if you have developed the skill. You can pray to your higher power if you feel so moved. However, just being aware of yourself and your surroundings is sufficient. This quiet time will give you the opportunity to reflect on your life and make significant plans for your future. Use it wisely.

Try to enjoy being alone.

Learn how it feels to be really alone. Turn off the TV, smart phone, or computer. Imagine, just you, alone somewhere with no one else around and no electronic connection.

Try lying on a beach or sitting on a rock overlooking a valley. Breathe deeply and enjoy the view. If you can't be in a different location, use your imagination. Reflect on who you are, where you have been, and where you want to go. Don't dwell on negativity, but rather, consider how lucky you are to be right here, right now.

Be grateful everyday.

Simply waking up in the morning should reinforce your desire to express gratitude. Be grateful for your life today because tomorrow is not guaranteed.

If you awoke in a house or apartment that has running water and electricity, be grateful. Probably, you don't need to start a fire for either warmth or light, or go outside to get water from a well like our ancestors did.

Be grateful for every breath you take, for every person in your life, for everything you have, and everything you are. Not everyone is as lucky as you are and you should celebrate your good fortune to be who you are.

Chapter Five

Make Better Choices

Take personal responsibility for your own actions.

Every day you have choices. You can choose to do or not do anything in your life. No one can make you do anything that you do not agree to do, unless, of course that other person has a gun to your head and is making you open the bank safe.

Short of that, however, no one can really make you do anything. The excuse of saying that someone else "made" you do something implies that you have no control over your actions. The first and most significant ability of a responsible person is to be able to control your actions.

Entrepreneurial Thinking is taking complete responsibility for your thoughts, the images you visualize, and the actions you take. In fact, Winston Churchill once said that, "The price of greatness is responsibility."

Everything in your life is a direct result of the choices you make. You choose your amount of debt, and how much money you make or don't make. You choose the status of your relationships. You choose your health, and your level of physical fitness. You choose your attitudes and behaviors. You and only you are in control of the quality of your life.

Remember that all actions have consequences.

For example, you can choose to get up and go to work or not. If you choose not to go to work, then you must accept the consequences of your actions. Those consequences could be the loss of that job, the loss of a place to live, the loss of providing for your family.

Every day, millions of people wake up and go to work at a job they dislike. They do so because they accept the financial responsibilities that they have for themselves and for their families.

These people are heroes and they deserve respect and admiration.

ENTREPRENEURIAL THINKING requires that you make the decision to do the right thing at the right time on an every day basis.

If you have a job, you must choose to go to work.

If you chose to get up and go to work at a job, then you have agreed to do the work assigned by your employer for the pay you have agreed to accept. Do the work you have agreed to be paid for. Cheating on your agreement by not doing the work is unethical. If you refuse to do the assigned job you are being paid for, then quit that job and find another one that you are willing to fulfill your work agreement

You should never badmouth your employer unless you are prepared to leave and find another job. No employer will tolerate a negative employee for very long. Remember that no one is irreplaceable. Consider if you pass away, another person will take your place at work or the employer will do without your activities. You need to bloom where you are planted and strive to be the loveliest flower in the garden of life.

Give a day's work for a day's pay.

Once you are at your job, you must give it your best. Since you have agreed to accept your employer's money in exchange for your time, you should strive to accomplish whatever your tasks might be. Be aware that these tasks probably will not always be fun, exciting, or challenging, but you need to do them anyway.

This doesn't mean that you should do anything illegal or unethical, but if you have been hired to clean toilets, make sure that you clean them to the best of your ability.

If you want a perfect example of this concept, go to You Tube and watch the latrine inspection scene in, "No Time for Sergeants," starring the late Andy Griffith. Watch how he cleaned the latrine. Don't feel compelled to make your toilet seat salute; this example is just for illustration.

You should always do the best you can; not for anyone else, but for yourself. Whatever you are doing right now is the gateway to your dreams.

You're learning to excel at everything in your life because you're excelling at what you're doing today. **ENTREPRENEURIAL THINKING** will help you to become a master of what you're doing today. To do so will fuel your improving your life and making it to the next level.

Never Stop Learning.

Just because you have a low-paying job doesn't mean that you should have no ambition. Go to college or a trade school to improve your likelihood of acquiring and maintaining a better job than you currently have.

For everyone, especially ones with the mindset of an Entrepreneur, education is a lifelong endeavor. You actually learn things all of the time. If you are going to be learning anyway, get college or vocational credits for learning. Get the credits so you can get a better job, or perhaps a raise. Find courses that will lead to professional certifications or a marketable degree.

After you have earned as many degrees as you think are necessary, feel free to take courses that feed your soul such as art or music. You can also take courses in subjects that simply help you understand your life and how to make it better, or to help you understand the world.

Be proactive in all areas of your life.

Entrepreneurial Thinking requires that in any given situation, you need to anticipate what might happen and prepare for contingencies. This way you will be able to head off most problems before they escalate. You never want to have to react to a preventable situation that you could have prepared for in the first place.

Things need to be done when they need to be done, not, necessarily, when you get around to them. If you plant a garden, you must get rid of the weeds before the weeds kill the plants you are planning to grow. In business, you need to make the phone calls as soon as you get the leads. Clear up a misunderstanding before it escalates. For example, build a storm-proof building before a hurricane can come by.

In relationships, you need to remember significant dates. An anniversary present or birthday card loses its impact if it arrives a week or more late. Or worse, if you have to be reminded of the dates because you have a memory like a steel sieve, your partner might wonder about your level of commitment and affection. Use reminders as needed.

Do things right the first time.

Never take a shortcut if it means shortchanging yourself or someone else. Shortcuts almost always leave out important steps that will then cause the expenditure of additional resources to correct the mistakes. Prevention and preparation are keys to ordered thinking like an entrepreneur.

It always helps to begin with the end in mind. Clearly identified goals and actions to accomplish these goals should be laid our as steps in the correct sequence of events needed for completion of the required task.

When trying to accomplish a specific task, use a Program Evaluation Review Technique called a PERT Chart. A PERT Chart is used by professional project managers in almost every industry. It is a way to structure tasks in the correct sequence to make sure that all required steps are accomplished in the order necessary to complete the process in the most efficient way possible.

Other fields call this sequence "story-boarding" where illustrations are used to show each step toward the finished product or production. Use whatever planning steps work best for you.

Make no excuses.

When faced with any task, you must give it your best shot. In "Star Wars," Yoda said it best, "Try not. Do or do not, there is no try."

If you give it your best shot and you still manage to mess it up, accept the responsibility of the mistake. You could always say something like, "Wow, that was a lot harder than I thought it was going to be."

Then, you need to figure out what happened. Focus on the parts that worked, figure out why you failed, and improve on the process. This will make it more likely for you to be able to do it correctly the next time.

ENTREPRENEURIAL THINKING includes the positive idea of always doing your best in everything you tackle. Learning how to do things better may be what you need to do. Be open to new ways to do things.

Never fear rejection.

Move forward. The person who rejected you might have simply been having a bad day. The rejection may have had nothing to do with you. People in sales have to go from rejection to rejection before finally finding the one person who believes that they will benefit from the product or service being offered. It is just a numbers game. Talk to 100 people, get ten appointments and make 1 sale.

Really successful sales people keep track of their numbers. That way when they do make the sale, they understand how much money they make per phone call. So if you make $5,000 on one sale and it started with those 100 phone calls, then you actually made $50.00 every time you called someone.

It becomes pretty easy to accept rejection 99 times knowing that the next time you'll make the $5,000 you made before. In this example, it is just a numbers game that one must accept as part of the work sequence. The key is to stay optimistic and never give up. Persistence always pays off in the long run.

Find a way to be self-reliant.

You may not want to live on a desert island, or be on any one of the reality shows that watch people trying to live in inhospitable environments. However, you should be self-sufficient enough that you can figure out simple things.

If water runs off of your roof and digs a hole in your yard, you should be able to figure out how to fix the problem using your own reasoning skills.

The bottom line is the simple fact that the only person you can truly rely on day-in and day-out 7 days a week, 24 hours a day, 365 days a year, is you.

"If it is to be, it is up to me." This anonymous quotation has been on posters and quoted in books since the 1950's. Self-reliance is one of the foundational concepts of **Entrepreneurial Thinking.**

This doesn't mean that you must do everything by yourself. If you can do something more profitable with your time then you can hire someone else to do some things. Consider hiring people as time savers. I'm not talking only about paying the teenager next door to cut your grass or wash your car.

Andrew Carnegie, the world's first documented Billionaire famously said, "I'd rather have one percent of the efforts of 100 people than 100% of my own."

Whenever possible, multiply your efforts by engaging people whose expertise exceeds your own. Just make sure that you are spending your time more productively.

If you're making $50,000 a year working for someone else, it doesn't make sense to hire someone who makes more money than you do to do a task that you could do yourself. This reflects poor time management on your part. Use your time and energy wisely.

Clean up your own messes.

All great people came into the world having someone else clean up their messy diapers. However, you should not get used to always having someone else around to clean up your messes.

ENTREPRENEURIAL THINKING requires you to take responsibility for everything you do either good or bad. You also should take the responsibility to clean up whatever you have messed up.

Cleaning up whatever you mess up includes apologizing to anyone who you did something negative to. It also includes understanding the results of your errors and taking the steps to correct the error and prevent it from reoccurring. If someone does clean up your messes for you, show heartfelt appreciation and reciprocate whenever possible.

If you are the member of a team, each of you should work towards the betterment of the team goals and help each other out as necessary. As such, you should always pull your own weight and not become an unnecessary burden to the team.

Avoid distractive driving: Never Tailgate and Never allow yourself to be tailgated.

One of the greatest motivators of **Entrepreneurial Thinking** is to be in control of your life. One example is in the skill of driving. Be aware of your surroundings and avoid distractions. No one wants to drive next to someone looking at a cell phone or driving with no hands while eating lunch.

Another distraction is tailgating the driver ahead of you. Being too close is dangerous to everyone in every vehicle nearby. By tailgating someone in front of you, you are allowing someone else to control whether you are in a wreck or not. Either pass the slowpoke if it is safe to do so or fall back and be patient. Driving on their bumper will not encourage the driver to go faster. Getting angry would be losing control of your actions.

Similarly, if you allow someone else to tailgate you, you are also risking being hit from behind if you stop suddenly. You may consider slowing down, so the speeder can safely pass. in order to be completely safe, if there is space to do so, simply pull off to the side of the road and stop to get rid of the tailgater.

Use time off the road to reflect on the general state of your life or simply look around and try to enjoy your surroundings while you let traffic pass you. You will avoid getting angry or being involved in a collision by letting someone else be tailgated by the idiot who had been following you too closely.

Tailgaters are clearly very aggressive drivers. As such, they could very well attempt to pass you, run head-on into another car, and involve you in a life-threatening collision because of their careless driving.

Entrepreneurial Thinking demands that you control every aspect of your life including your driving habits. Controlling your own safety and the safety of those in your vehicle should certainly be in the forefront of your actions behind the wheel.

Make a good decision about having someone else do something for you.

It's difficult to cut your own hair properly. To demonstrate, here is a story about how to decide who to choose as a hair stylist.

A person moved to a small town that only had two hair stylists. They met with hair stylist one and that person's hair looked perfectly styled. Then they met with hair stylist two whose hair looked horrible.

They thought that they should go to the first hair stylist because that person's hair looked perfect. However, upon careful consideration, they decided that each hair stylist had to go to the other one to have their hair styled.

Therefore, the one with the horribly styled hair was the stylist that perfectly styled the other stylist's hair and vice versa. Upon that consideration, the stylist who did the better job was the one whose hair looked the worst.

Entrepreneurial Thinking means to make good decisions about who to hire to do things for you that you can't do yourself. Be observant and get references.

Chapter Six

Learn How to
Do Some Things
Yourself

Learn how tools work.

You don't need to build a house to learn how a hammer works and that nails can hold things together. Get a how-to book on the use of common tools or take an extension course at your local technical school.

You could just pick up a hammer and start banging at things. Just make sure you don't destroy anything important like your smart phone or computer.

Go to some hardware stores and check out their do-it-yourself seminars. Even if the seminar is on building something you may never want to build, what they are demonstrating will at least present ideas of how a task can be done.

Use this knowledge when hiring others to do the actual work. **Entrepreneurial Thinking** also means that the more you know about various subjects, the more You can evaluate other people's ability to perform certain tasks. If you are generally familiar with the process of doing things, you are less likely to be ripped off by unethical contractors.

Not everyone is ethical so you need to protect yourself as much as possible. Also, you might find that you actually enjoy doing some projects yourself. Sometimes it is fun to do a project yourself because it can make you feel more creative if you accomplished what you started.

Be wary of unethical contractors.

Once when I wanted my house painted, I ended up with an unethical contractor. I wanted someone to paint my house and he agreed to meet me at my house at a certain time to go over the details.

He never showed up. I had taken a day off work and waited all day. I tried to call him multiple times but he didn't answer. I felt that if anyone fails to be responsible enough to meet at the beginning of a project, how can they be trusted to complete the project on time and within budget?

Finally, late in the afternoon he answered the phone. I told him that I didn't want him to do the project because he didn't even have the courtesy to contact me. He was very upset.

Several days later I received a notice in the mail that I had a contractor's lien on my property for $4,000 for failure to pay for work done on my property. I had to go to court to file a response that he had never shown up to nor did he actually do any work.

If I had not responded to the lien notice, I may have been forced by the court to pay for work that was actually never done.

Lessons learned: have a signed contract and make sure the contractor is licensed, bonded, and insured. Also, make sure that the contractor can provide you with positive references before you agree to hire him or her to do anything you don't have the time or the skill to do within the required time.

The signed contract needs to include the following items:

1. The details of the tasks required to complete the project including the total scope of the work.
2. The total price to complete the project.
3. The time to complete the work.
4. If you choose to do so then include a bonus if the contractor completes the project on time.
5. If the contractor agrees, then include a penalty if the project is not completed on time.
6. Wording that details that the contractor is responsible for obtaining any required permits.
7. Wording that details the proof of insurance that the contractor must have in order to do the project.

Buy Yourself a set of tools.

Buy one set of good tools that will perform the tasks that you are most likely to have the time and ability to accomplish. When you do go to the seminars at the hardware store, choose the tools they demonstrate that seem to work for the types of projects that interest you to do yourself.

You don't need to spend thousands of dollars for tools that would allow you to work on bulldozers when you drive a Nissan Altima. However, if you do drive a Nissan Altima, and you want to work on it, you will need a set of metric tools. Learn the difference.

Choosing some tools to keep over time will allow you to be constructive when you need or want to feel that way. Just make sure that you don't purchase too many tools that you will never have the ability to use.

Learn to do some simple repairs yourself.

You should be able to do some simple repairs around your house rather than have to call in an expert for every little thing. Learn when it is time to call an expert, before you destroy anything beyond repair. If you do call an expert and you want to learn what they are doing don't be afraid to watch what they do.

Don't ask too many questions. Sometimes the prices you pay are based on your level of interference.

Labor charge: $20.00 per hour

If you watch: $25.00 per hour

If you help: $50.00 per hour

That was a joke! ☺

You don't need to try to do everything yourself, or even learn everything. When you can do something more productive and more profitable with your time, pay the expert what they charge and leave them to do their work.

If you can do a task and save money by not hiring someone else, you should do so only if you don't have something else to do with your time that would make you more money. **Entrepreneurial Thinking** requires that you should use your time for your best financial benefit whenever possible.

Learn to Wash and repair your own clothes.

The concept is pretty simple: put dirty clothes and laundry detergent in the washing machine. After it cuts off, place the clothes in the dryer. **HOORAY!** clean clothes! Wash dark clothes in cold water and light-colored clothes in warm water. The cold water helps reduce fading so that your dark clothes look better longer.

Once you take the clothes out of the dryer, you should hang them on a hanger or fold them up and put them away. Do it NOW, not in a few minutes, next week, or next year. Piles of clothes not put away are just clutter.

If something is torn, fix it now or throw it away. If you can't repair it tomorrow or next week, take it somewhere to be fixed. If not, realize that the item is un-wearable and throw it away.

Entrepreneurial Thinking implies that you should do things when they need to be done, not when you get around to it. This is true for everything that you need to do in your life.

The next few recommendations confirm the importance of doing things when they need to be done in order to make your life better.

Learn how to use a needle and thread.

The simplest repair is to replace a button. Just look at the piece of clothing where the button was and put it back in the same place.

It's better if you can put the same button back on If you can find it or keep it when it comes off, If not, try to use a button of the same or similar color. You don't want to have one black button on your white shirt. That would just look tacky.

You will find that when using a needle and thread that one indispensable accessory is a thimble. You can find a sewing kit that will contain needles and threads that can be used for most reasons at several stores.

Sometimes, when you buy clothing, what you purchased requires some modification to fit you well. If possible, try to have the store where you bought the clothing to alter it so it will fit better.

When you purchase clothing online, you will probably have to do the alteration yourself or try to send it back for a refund. The problem is that it will usually cost you to pay the postage to send it back. Therefore, you might prefer to do the alteration yourself so the clothing will fit properly. Or, you can avoid on-line items that do not allow for free returns.

Learn how to iron your dress clothing.

You may decide that it is worth whatever they charge to send your dress clothing to the laundry. However, you need to understand what it takes to accomplish the task. Besides, you might really need to iron a piece of dress clothing for a special event because you forgot to pick up your laundry on time.

There are two basic types of ironing devices, a flat iron and a steam iron. Both types can help you make your dress clothing look neat and proper. Most of the time you also need to use an ironing board so that the heat from the iron does not damage another flat surface that you use to iron your clothing on.

Learn how to prepare your edible food.

No, really! Learn how to use the stove and the oven, not just the microwave and the toaster. You may surprise yourself by actually being able to eat something that you prepared yourself.

Consider to buy a regional or generic cookbook. Then, try to use one new recipe a month for a year. Being able to cook for yourself and someone else might improve your relationship with the other person. Cooking gives the creator a sense of accomplishment. You can just stick to the basics.

Besides, the ability to cook edible food may become important if you have financial problems and cannot afford to always eat out. Also, being able to cook or simply prepare breakfast on a daily basis will usually help you save time every day. This will allow you to be able to begin to start your day more rapidly than having to go to a restaurant or wait in the take-out line every morning.

Learn how to read maps.

Learn how to read maps, not just road maps, but a topographical map of the land. You need to understand contour lines and recognize trails and roads. The closer contour lines are together, the steeper the hill. Trails and roads are marked differently and you need to identify them.

GPS devices or Smart Phone Apps can get you from where you are to where you want to go. Usually, they take you via major roadways or Interstates.

However, if you want to enjoy the landscape and views of the area you are driving through, road maps are very helpful. Many road maps have dotted line roadways that show you where the scenic byways are so that you can see the beautiful and picturesque area landscapes.

Another kind of map is a map of the waterways. Driving a boat is quite different than driving a car. If you're near the coastline, you need to be able to read where the shoals and sand bars are. It's much harder to walk back when you wreck your boat that when you wreck your car.

Learn how to use a compass.

Understand that the compass points to magnetic north, not true north. If you can both read a map and use a compass, you will be able to do some back country hiking without depending on electronics.

Electronics have the annoying habit of failing at the most inconvenient time. Also, if you accidentally drop any electronic device into water, do not be surprised that it will stop working. Electronics and water do not get along.

Learn basic navigation skills.

You should be able to use the east-west movement of the sun to walk in a northerly direction. You should, at least, be able to recognize the North Star.

If you are hiking through the wilderness, understanding the directions you are going will help you return to your starting point. Getting lost in the woods is not the result that anyone should accept when they are enjoying the outdoors.

If you are driving a boat through unfamiliar waterways you will need to be able to return to the place you started. To really improve your ability to navigate, take a boating class from a certified instructor.

Being able to clearly understand any task you choose to do is an important concept that corresponds with the mindset of **ENTREPRENEURIAL THINKING.**

Understand basic self-defense.

Take a class in self-defense from your local police department or YMCA. Or you could take a karate class from one of the many karate schools that most communities have. You don't need to be Bruce Lee or Jet Li, but you should be able to move well enough to protect yourself, or to at least get out of the way if someone attacks you.

The preference is to be able to diffuse the situation and avoid a physical confrontation if possible. But do not allow yourself to be a victim if you are attacked. This is another reason to be in reasonably good shape. If nothing else, being able to get away from someone trying to assault you would truly be the preferable goal rather than trying to fight with anyone. Jogging is a good exercise to get in shape to get away from being assaulted.

Learn how to shoot a gun.

Don't try to be James Bond or Laura Croft. Take lessons on weapon's safety and how to shoot a pistol with a two-handed stance. Many law enforcement agencies have beginning gun safety training sessions. Check with your local agencies to see if one is available.

You need to become familiar enough so that if the need ever arises, you will feel comfortable handling and using a weapon.

Some celebrities that have carried a permitted weapon when they go out in public have said that they feel differently about other people when they carry a gun. They said that by carrying a weapon, it made them more suspicious of people around them. They kept wondering who else in the crowd had a weapon.

You should never threaten or even point at anyone with a gun, even one that you think is unloaded. Many people have killed their friends with an "empty" gun. "I didn't know the gun was loaded" may or may not work as a defense in a courtroom, but it won't bring your friend back. Assume all guns are loaded.

Never leave a gun out where children may find it. The news is too common where a child found a loaded gun and shot someone either accidentally or on purpose. In one case a 10-year-old took a gun to school and shot their friend because of an argument.

If you do choose to have weapons in your home, teach gun safety to your children as soon as they are old enough to understand what a weapon is. But still, in your own home, keep all weapons under lock and key, at all times.

When you handle a weapon, the following instructions will keep you and everyone around you safe:

1. Make certain that you know how to use your weapon safely. This is where safety training comes in.

2. Always keep your finger off of the trigger until you are ready to fire your weapon.

3. Always keep your firearm unloaded both in storage and while you are transporting it.

4. Always keep your firearm pointed in a safe direction.

5. Always wear eye and ear protection.

6. Always store your firearm where it is not accessible by any unauthorized person.

7. Always store ammunition separately from your firearm.

8. Always make certain that your firearm is clean and free from mechanical defects in order to be certain that it is safe to operate.

9. NEVER use alcohol or any drug that can interfere with your mental ability before or during the use of your firearm.

Chapter Seven

Improve Your Health

Strive to be healthy.

Make a conscious effort to choose the healthier option whenever presented with choices. For example, use the stairs rather than the elevator if you are going up or down less than 10 flights of stairs. Also, consider to have a low-fat sandwich instead of burgers and fries. You probably understand what you really should do. You just need to make the correct choices in order to actually do it.

ENTREPRENEURIAL THINKING encourages you to be able to do everything you need to do in order to improve your life. The healthier you are, the easier it will be to do everything you need to do on a daily basis in order to make all aspects of your life better.

Use hand sanitizer to sterilize and protect yourself.

Use hand sanitizer after you wash your hands, before you handle food, especially food you are going to eat. Many people started using some hand sanitizer after COVID became a pandemic but not necessarily as often as it could help to protect them from other infections. You could choose to use it on a daily basis as it could help to protect you from other infections.

If someone around you is coughing or sneezing, use a little of the hand sanitizer on the inside of your nose and on your upper lip. A dab in your ears might also help keep infectious germs out of your body as well.

Hand sanitizer may not protect you completely, but it will certainly help reduce the likelihood of contracting any kind of communicable disease. As always, reducing the frequency of contact with communicable diseases will continue to keep your immune system from becoming less able to fight off negative health issues.

Be Aware that a specific combination of Some Vitamins and minerals can Improve Your Immune System

The following combination of these specific vitamins and minerals with their specific strengths can provide you with the necessary nutrition that can significantly improve your immune system. Usually, you should take every one of these two or three times a day with a meal.

Take one 1000mg of Vitamin C. Take two 5,000 mcg of Vitamin B12. Take two 125 mcg of Vitamin D3. Take one 50 mg of Zinc.

Other Vitamins and supplements will also help you improve your health.

Choose a single multi-vitamin dietary supplement based on your gender and age. Typically, these single dietary supplements do not include the maximum amount of every vitamin or mineral that is necessary according to the FDA regulations.

In order to consume at least the recommended quantity of every vitamin and supplement, you need to add the missing amounts in other pills. Some of the additional vitamins and supplements you probably need to take are as follows: Vitamin E, Vitamin A, Potassium, Calcium, and Magnesium, You can do your own research to decide if there are any more vitamins or supplements that you need to take.

For example, if you are having urinary track issues, you can add a Cranberry pill which allegedly helps those issues. Some people believe that if you are having joint problems that Glucosamine/Chondroitin will help you. Similarly, if you are having problems with inflammation, Turmeric Curcumin is supposed to help. Just choose the supplements that you think you need.

As always, if you are taking any prescription medications, you need to check with your physician or pharmacist. Check with these professionals in order to determine whether or not any of the vitamins or supplements you are taking will reduce or cancel the benefit of the prescription medications you are taking. **Thinking like an Entrepreneur** includes doing the right thing at the right time for the correct reason. Clearly, consistently taking whatever you need to take to get healthier is always the right thing to do.

Understand the concept of optimal health.

You need to understand that the apparent absence of disease does not automatically equate to being in optimal health. There is a graphic that explains this health-illness continuum. It looks like this:

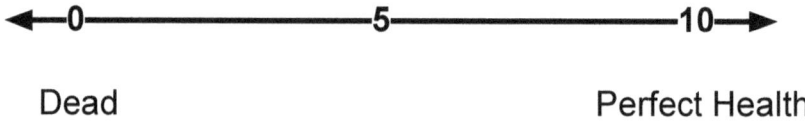

Dead   Perfect Health

On this graph, most people are somewhere around a 5. The problem is that most people don't start taking care of themselves until they have some kind of traumatic health crisis.

How many people do you know of that had a heart attack in their late 40s and then changed their diet and started on an exercise program. How much better off would they have been if they had started taking care of themselves before the crisis.

Diseases can be classified as vertical or horizontal. Heart attacks, strokes or other critical diseases that put you in bed are horizontal diseases. You have no doubt that you have a problem when you have one of these health issues. The problem is that every disease is a vertical disease before it becomes a horizontal disease.

For example, heart attacks don't just happen out of the blue. Obviously, before a person had a heart attack, there was some kind of health problem that actually caused the heart attack.

Other diseases can be vertical for a very long time before the disease becomes a horizontal disease. According to 2022 US government statistics nearly 70% of Americans are overweight. According to the CDC over 120 million people have diabetes or prediabetes. Clearly diabetes is a lifestyle problem and, as such, is mostly preventable.

Take the steps to reduce your chances of getting cancer.

According to research, the most common type of cancer in the United States is Melanoma also known as skin cancer. Melanoma is caused by the exposure to Ultraviolet light which is primarily sunlight but sometimes even tanning bed lights. Getting sunburned often without using sunscreen is the principle cause.

In 1994 Ted Turner announced that he had skin cancer when he was talking to a graduation class. He recommended to the graduating students that they should put on sunscreen and wear a hat.

Another significant type of cancer that causes frequent deaths is lung cancer. Most of the people who get lung cancer are smokers. The second set of people who get lung cancer are ones who are exposed to second-hand smoke from smokers.

Unfortunately, in 2015, the Star Trek Star, Leonard Nimoy was diagnosed with COPD which caused his death. Before he passed away, he announced that he had COPD because he had smoked for many years, a habit he had given up almost three decades earlier.

Smoking can also cause cancer of the larynx, mouth and throat, On some TV commercials advertising some anti-smoking medicines, they frequently show someone who has larynx cancer and is speaking through some electronic vocal device. Smoking is harmful and kills. If you have never smoked, just don't. If you are a smoker, quit. Be in control of your habits. Don't let your habits control you.

According to research, Overweight and Obesity are associated with at least 13 types of cancer, These cancers include uterine cancer, breast cancer, colorectal cancer and several others. Clearly maintaining your best weight and muscle mass will help you reduce the likelihood of many types of cancer.

Some infectious diseases can cause cancer. Research has shown that Human papillomavirus (HPV), Hepatitis B virus and Hepatitis C virus can cause different types of cancer. Some of the cancers that can be caused by these diseases include liver cancer, cervical cancer, as well as cancer of the vagina, vulva, penis, and anus.

Luckily, all of these specific diseases currently have available vaccines. By being properly vaccinated, you could help reduce the likehood of acquiring these diseases. Therefore, not getting any of these diseases, it will reduce the likelihood of getting any of the types of cancers that they can cause.

Other research explains how cancer cells can multiply if any are already anywhere in your body. According to this research, basically, the more sugar you have in your diet, the more likely cancer cells will increase in size and quantity.

Take care of yourself first.

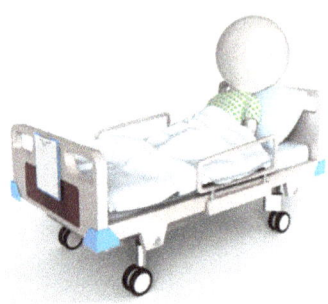

Taking care of your own physical and mental health is not being selfish. However, if you don't take care of your own health first, then you will not be able to take care of anyone else. It is hard to take care of your loved ones from a hospital bed or if you are in a mental health facility.

Exercise every day.

You don't have to spend 5 hours in the gym or run a marathon every day. You can do just a few simple exercises that will get your muscles firing and your heart pumping.

You don't need to spend a fortune on equipment either. Crunches and push-ups are free and so are walking and running. Just make sure to use proper form. Be cautious of running on hard surfaces; you don't want to have your knees replaced before you're 50. That happened to two different people I know. They ran a lot but had to have their knees replaced.

If you do a set of crunches or planks every morning you will do more than most people. This is another case where **Entrepreneurial Thinking** whose philosophy includes taking care of yourself is helpful. Other types of calisthenics like squat-thrusts, side straddle hops, or others will also help. The more you can do, the healthier you will become

One of the tenants of **Entrepreneurial Thinking** is to be consistent with all goals. The key to a great exercise program is also to be consistent. It does no good to exercise once a month or every once in a while.

Planks or pushups   Side straddle hops

If you're doing planks go ahead and do a few push-ups. If you're doing the planks properly, you're already in the basic push-up position. The planks are strengthening your entire core; abdominals, external obliques, and your hips. The push-ups will add a workout for your pectorals, triceps, biceps, and your deltoids.

Consider buying two or three sets of dumbbells to focus on your biceps and triceps. To start with, pick a weight you can do easily like 10 or 15 pounds. Then get another set 5 or 10 pounds heavier so that you can continually progress. Get a third set another 5 or 10 pounds heavier to really give yourself a goal.

According to personal trainers, don't get the adjustable dumbbells that you have to change the weight of. The little bit of money you save will be totally wasted because of the time it takes to keep changing the weights on the bar.

Also, don't get a full barbell set. In addition to the insane amount of space it will take to store them when you aren't using them, their sheer size and cumbersome nature will make it much less likely that you will actually use them often enough to make the inconvenience worthwhile.

Now that you have a few weight choices you can use a set for your lunges. Properly done, lunges target your quadriceps, glutes, and your hamstrings.

Except for the walking or running, you can do all of these exercises in the comfort and convenience of your own bedroom. You can do the crunches even before you get out of bed. The planks and push-ups can be done on the floor next to your bed. Keep the dumbbells just inside your closet so you can do your curls and triceps extensions in front of the mirror on your closet door.

In the length of time it would have taken you to get dressed and driven to the gym, you have now completed a basic fitness regimen that will give you all the energy you need to get out the door and take on the world.

You also could have saved about $600 to $1200 a year on costs of going to a gymnasium. You could then place that amount you saved into your IRA or other retirement account. Be sure to remember this when you read the chapter on personal finance.

I once knew an elderly man who was a retired World War II air force pilot. He said that he still did a 15 to 30 minute set of calisthenics every morning. He lived to be 99 years old. He also did not have any dementia or other mental problems. Clearly, the concept of exercising every day works to keep you healthy and extends your life.

As always, **Entrepreneurial Thinking** is the mindset to take the steps necessary to improve all aspects of your life every day.

Understand how your body works.

You already know about the fun parts. You should remember something from the basic health class you might have had in high school. That's not enough. You need to learn about what happens when you exercise. You also need to understand what are your basic nutritional requirements and how your musculoskeletal system works to hold your body together.

You need to know what you need to do to help your body remain healthy. One useful bit of information is the fact that one pound of fat equates to approximately 4,000 calories. So if you are trying to lose weight you will need to eat 4,000 calories less than your body needs to maintain your current activity level, or you need to increase your activity level to burn an additional 4,000 calories.

You can use any one of the free calorie calculators available on the internet to find out how best to accomplish your goals.

Here is the formula to calculate how many calories you need to consume every day for your body to maintain your existing weight.

For Men, $(66+(6.3 \times \text{weight in pounds})+(12.9 \times \text{height in inches} - (6.8 \times \text{Age in years})) \times 1.3$

If a 40 year old man is 5'10" and weighs 180 pounds, here is the number of calories he needs to consume to maintain his existing weight.

$(66 + (6.3 \times 180) + (12.9 \times 70) - (6.8 \times 40)) \times 1.3$

$(66 + 1134 + 903 - 272) \times 1.3$

$1831 \times 1.3 = \textbf{2,280 calories per day}$

For Women, $655 + (4.3 \times \text{weight in pounds}) + (4.7 \times \text{height in inches} - (4.7 \times \text{Age in years}) \times 1.3$.

If a 30 year old woman is 5'5" and weighs 150 pounds, here is the number of calories she needs to consume to maintain her existing weight.

$(655 + (4.3 \times 150) + (4.7 \times 65) - (4.7 \times 30)) \times 1.3$

$(655 + 645 + 305 - 141) \times 1.3$

$1464 \times 1.3 = \textbf{1,903 calories per day}$

According to some physical research, if you do not consume enough protein on a daily basis, your system could dissolve some of your soft internal organs in order to have sufficient protein in your blood. In other words, your body could dissolve parts of your heart, liver, kidneys, intestines, and potentially other parts of your digestive system.

The formula to calculate how many grams of protein you need to consume in order to prevent your body from dissolving your organs is as follows:

Your full body weight in pounds, divided by 20 and multiplied by 7. In other words, if you weigh 180 pounds,

180 divided by 20 is 9. Multiply 9 × 7 so the minimum number of grams of protein you must consume every day is 63.

One thing that most people don't clearly understand is the internal electrical connections within the human body that controls all bodily functions. The nerves that radiate throughout your body send electrical signals to all of your internal organs to tell your organs to do what is necessary to function properly. When your internal organs consistently function properly, you will likely improve your health

Interferences in the electrical signals can have negative results in your health. Just like telephone and computer wiring that still exist throughout the world, disturbances in the wiring can disrupt effective communication. The main focus in Chiropractic bodily adjustments is to improve the nerve communication in your body so that your organs get the correct signals in order to function properly.

If you clearly understand how your body works, then you can make good decisions to improve your overall health. As always, **ENTREPERNEAL THINKING** is the basic concept to help you to consistently make good decisions for every aspect of your life.

Understand the importance of getting enough sleep every day.

Sleep has an important role In regulating hormones, metabolism, and inflammation, all of which can contribute to chronic disease. Also, having enough sleep provides improved physical performance, better reaction time, better endurance and muscle recovery.

More benefits of getting enough sleep include improved cognitive function, lower risk of chronic diseases, and improved overall health and wellness. Also, sleep helps consolidate memories and enhance neural connections, leading to improved creativity.

Research has found that professional athletes who get adequate sleep have better performance, less fatigue, and lower risk of injury.

The things you can do to improve you sleep are as follows: Establishing a regular sleep schedule, creating a relaxing sleep environment, and avoiding stimulants and electronics.

The tips for creating a relaxing sleep environment includes using blackout curtains or eye masks to block out light. Also, using earplugs or white noise machines will reduce negative, objectionable noise. You should also choose comfortable bedding and pillows, including perhaps, a neck roll. Avoid the light simulates like television and cell phones.

A consistent bedtime routine can signal the body that it's time to wind down and prepare for sleep. It will also help to regulate the sleep-wake cycle.

Verify your healthy numbers.

Have regular checkups. Know what your blood pressure, blood sugar, and cholesterol levels are. Understand how your height and weight calculate into your Body Mass Index and what those numbers should be in order for you to be considered healthy.

According to the latest medical wisdom, your blood pressure should be 120/80 or slightly lower. If your lower number ever gets over 95, you might need to call your doctor.

Blood sugar is the way your body gets fuel for all of your bodily functions. Your blood sugar is measured by the amount of glucose in your blood after fasting. A normal fasting blood glucose level is between 70 and 99 milligram per deciliter of blood, or 1/1000th of a gram per 1/10th of a liter. Too much sugar can be a sign of diabetes.

Cholesterol is a waxy substance that exists in the blood. It is produced by the liver and found in certain foods. It is needed to make vitamin D and some hormones, build cell walls, and create bile salts that help you digest fat. The amount of cholesterol in the bloodstream is also tested after fasting.

Your total cholesterol should be between 100 and 199 milligrams per deciliter. This breaks down to the three major types; HDL, LDL, and VLDL.

HDL is the good cholesterol and you should have over 39 mg per HDL. According to ATP-III guidelines, HDL cholesterol over 59 mg per dl can help reduce your risk of coronary heart disease. LDL is bad cholesterol and you should have an LDL level of under 99 mg per dl. VLDL is very bad cholesterol and you should have no more than 40 mg of VLDL per dl.

Body Mass Index is calculated by your weight in kilograms divided by the square of your height in meters. A BMI of 18.5 to 24.9 is normal.

Keep your teeth clean.

Dental hygiene is the forefront of many health issues. There are several chronic conditions that are associated with poor oral hygiene. These include Alzheimer's, Heart Disease, Diabetes, Pancreatic Cancer, Osteoporosis and others.

There is a sign in my dentist's office that says, "You don't have to floss all your teeth every day; only the ones you want to keep." Taking care of all areas of your life is included in the concept of **Entrepreneurial Thinking**.

Be wary of alcohol.

More people are addicted to alcohol than to all other drugs combined. The health benefits purported of having a glass of wine can be achieved by eating fruits and practicing deep breathing.

Social drinking can be a trap if you are not careful. If you ever get so drunk that you can't remember what you did, that's not a good thing. So, did you take that $500.00 out of the ATM? If so, what did you do with it?

Alcohol can be a problem. Do you have a relative who always gets too drunk at family gatherings? If so, the tendency to drink too much could potentially be in your DNA.

You may have heard someone who no longer drinks say something like this as to why they stopped drinking, "I didn't get into trouble every time I had something to drink. But, every time I got into trouble, it was when I had too much to drink." Or something like, "I really liked the buzz, but I hated the drunk."

The trouble with drinking too much is that it is pervasive and yet society tends to accept it as normal. In the comics, Andy Capp has a drinking problem, but millions of people laugh at him every day.

Other comic strip characters have alcohol problems. In Hi and Lois, their next-door neighbor's nickname is Thirsty because he drinks too much. In many strips of this cartoon series, Thirsty's wife is complaining about his drinking because of his negative actions. In Beetle Bailey, the General frequently has too much to drink.

Many TV shows and movies portray alcoholics for laughs while others promote alcohol usage as popular and even sophisticated. Think of James Bond with his martini as "shaken not stirred." In any case alcohol usage and ruin families and business relationships, damage one's character, and leave one broke.

Entrepreneurial Thinking means to be in control of your life. Alcohol actually changes the brain's chemistry and interferes with higher order thinking such as decision making. As such, decisions made while impaired are usually not particularly good.

In the Spike Channel's old series "1000 Ways To Die" alcohol related deaths were the most prominent reasons people died in that show. One guy was drinking while he was running a piece of heavy equipment with a large heavy roller that was compressing the dirt. He jumped off the equipment and ran into the nearby porta-potty. He forgot to engage the brake before he got off and the machine rolled forward and destroyed the porta-potty with him inside of it, killing him

Whether to drink or not is a personal decision. You might be one of the millions of people who have a drink or two with your friends and stop drinking before you become drunk. If that is the case enjoy your social drinking just don't drink and drive.

On the other hand, if you are one of the millions of people who regularly get so drunk you can't remember what you did or who you did it with, do yourself and everyone else a favor, stop drinking. Drinking until you throw up is not normal, no matter how many people you know who do it.

Stop drinking before you go to jail with a Driving Under the Influence, DUI, or DWI, Driving While Intoxicated arrest. Or worse, stop drinking before you kill someone else, or kill yourself by driving while you're drunk. Even if you survive a wreck, you will have the mental trauma of the event and you might be arrested.

You don't have to make a big deal out of it by announcing to anyone within earshot of your decision to not drink. After you stop drinking and are offered a drink and you should just politely decline. A simple "no thank you" should be sufficient.

You can still have a good time, go out with your friends and, if you choose, have virgin cocktails or non-alcoholic beer. Be the designated driver to make sure that you and your friends get home safely.

The following diseases are related to excessive alcohol consumption:

- Diabetes
- Pancreatitis
- Anemia
- Platelet count reduction
- Heart Disease
- AFIB

- Osteoporosis
- Seizures
- Dementia

Most of these diseases are related to the fact that alcohol consumption affects liver health. All nutrients first go through the liver before being processed and sent to other organs in the body.

If you need help quitting, there are support groups available. Alcoholics Anonymous, community centers, some church groups and others will stand by your decision and give you needed support and reassurance. If someone in your family or a close friend has an alcoholic problem, you can seek support with organizations like Al-Anon that provides suggestions and support for dealing with the problem.

Don't mix some over-the-counter and prescription drugs.

Some over the counter medicines do not mix well with prescription drugs. Remember what happened to the celebrity, Heath Ledger. He combined too many O.T.C. medicines and prescription drugs and accidentally killed himself. Check with your pharmacist for interactions and side effects.

You have probably heard about the opioid problem in the world. Opioids are very powerful pain killers that are available when an individual has extreme pain. They are prescribed to help people overcome the pain from major surgeries and other physical trauma. They are also very addictive.

When Michael Jackson's hair caught on fire during the Infamous Pepsi commercial, he started taking opioids. Eventually, he became so addicted to pain medication he had his personal physician provide him with even stronger types until he finally overdosed and died.

Years ago, Elvis Presley took stimulants to get him up for performances and then had to have sedatives to relax him so he could get some rest. This artificial stimulant to sedative rollercoaster finally took it's toll and he died of an overdose.

As with alcohol and prescription medications or over the counter drugs, be careful mixing them with any other medication. Pay attention to the warnings on the labels. To be safe, check with your pharmacist or physician.

There is a scene in the movie "10" where Dudley Moore's character took pain pills because of dental surgery and started drinking when he got home.

When the police showed up at his house the officer told him that pain pills and alcohol don't mix. To which the totally wasted character slurred, "You could'a fooled me."

When all else fails, read the directions.

Never do illegal drugs.

You know the excuses, "everybody's doing them" and "it's just for medicinal purposes." But most illegal drugs have an insidious addictive side that will steal your soul, destroy your mind, and poison your body.

You need to understand the mental negativity related with use of illegal drugs. They all create mental instability as well as unrealistic expectations about yourself and the world. Taking them can set you up for failure. Besides jail time will not look good on your resume'. Just don't do it!

Alcohol and drugs that waste time and energy are anti-entrepreneurial thinking

All clear-headed entrepreneurs understand that the most valuable thing that you possesses is your time. Your time is all you have. What you choose to do with your time today will determine your quality of life for the rest of your life. There are no re-takes in real life.

Everyone has the same twenty-four hours per day. If you are frequently recovering from drugs or alcohol for the first several hours of the morning, that time is wasted and can never be recovered.

Over the course of a lifetime, even two or three mornings a week where you sit around waiting to feel better before you get to your tasks at hand can add up to many wasted years. Then when you are in your fifties or older, you might try to figure out where your dreams and ambitions went. You might discover that many times they simply vanished into the wasted years you spent waiting to try to feel better after a night of over-indulging.

Entrepreneurial Thinking demands that you focus on your tasks that you have defined that will take you towards your goals. Any time spent that does not take you forward towards your goals is time you could have made better use of. You cannot work to make your life better if you are too strung out or hung-over to function.

Chapter Eight

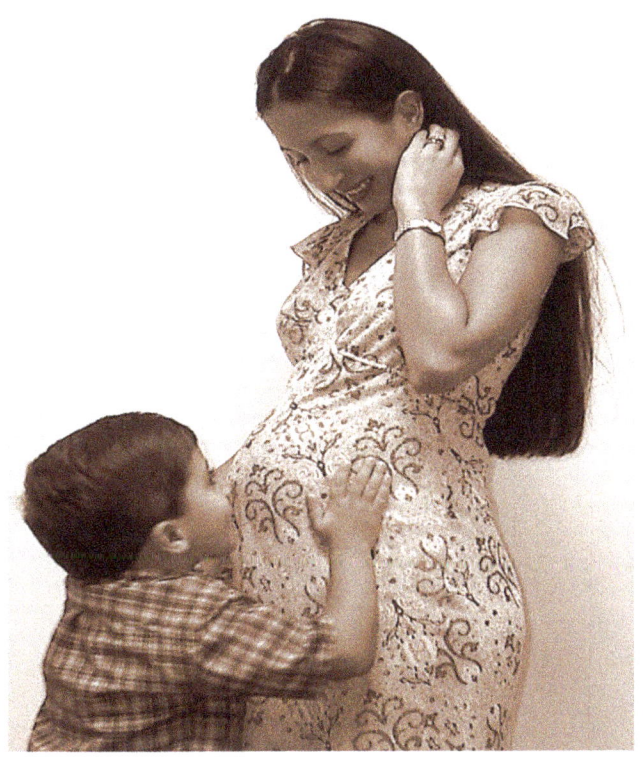

Improve Your
Relationships

Fall in love deeply, madly, truly and completely: How Successful Romantic Relationships Last

In true love, hold nothing back. Only then can you find real joy. Many people go into a relationship with one foot out of the door because of a fear of commitment. What if I get hurt? What if...what if...? This is no way to build a lifetime relationship.

You build relationships by keeping romance alive. Sporadically write a love note and slip it in your partner's jacket. It doesn't have to be a Shakespearean sonnet; just a simple "I Love You" will work. You could even call their cell phone when you know they won't answer and leave a loving voicemail. Something like, "I was just thinking about you and thought I'd tell you again how much I love you." Even a text with some significant emoji's will do wonders for building your relationship.

This shouldn't be perceived as a task or job to be done every day. Spontaneity and surprise will go further to help your loved one understand how special they are and how important they are to you.

When you go out together, you should hold hands. You don't need to be all over each other so that passers-by shout at you to "Get a Room." Just hold each other's hand. Be the first one to initiate the gesture and your partner will be pleasantly surprised. After all, we communicate love and caring by touching.

Why is it that some marriages only last mere hours while others endure for decades? To answer that question, one needs only to look at the some of the main reasons for divorce. Whether stresses around money, child-rearing, careers, or something as nebulous as "irreconcilable differences," the reason almost always boils down simply to a lack of communication.

Communication is simple, but it's not easy. Say what you mean and mean what you say is a very simple, concept However, again, it's not always easy to do. Make sure that the listener understands what you actually said. Clarity is important in all things. Honesty saves time.

However, let's look at this situation: Start with a seemingly innocuous question that nearly every woman has asked her significant other as they prepare to go out for the evening: "Honey, does this dress make me look fat?" How can a loving, caring husband or partner possibly answer that question with anything resembling complete honesty? This is especially problematic if his wife is, for whatever the reason, not a perfect size 7, or 5, or whatever the current media representation of what the perfect woman should look like.

So, what is the real question? The real question is a variation on one or more of these themes. Each of which is based on the insecurity that everyone has to some degree:

A. Do you still love me?

B. Do you still find me attractive?

C. When we go out tonight will you pay attention to me?

D. Can I count on you to make me feel special?

E. Will you find someone else tonight that you would rather be with?

F. Will you be critical of my choices tonight?

G. Will you come home with me tonight?

What is the proper answer to such a query? The response should be something along these lines:

"Darling, you look great. I love you very much. I know we're going to have a great time tonight. I can't wait to spend this evening with you." This should be accompanied with an appropriate hug and a kiss as emphasis.

The preceding exchange should in no way be confused with a similar question by the husband. Which usually goes something like this: "I'm ready to go. Do you like what I'm wearing?" There is most likely no hidden meaning. He probably means exactly what he has said.

If her response is, "You're not wearing that are you?" Then, to avoid further arguments and hurt feelings on both parts, he should immediately change his clothes. This should continue multiple times if necessary, until her response is something like, "Well, I guess that looks okay. I'm ready to leave whenever you are."

To avoid this situation, both parties should take a long look in the mirror. Many evenings and events have been ruined with misunderstandings over clothing or similar irritations. Make sure both of you agree on where you are going beforehand. Not everyone likes surprises. With food communications, problems can be solved early. Now the happy couple can leave their house or hotel room if they are out of town and can have a pleasant evening together.

One of the easiest ways to say "I Love You" to your significant other is to spend quality time together. Clear your schedule and do something that your partner enjoys, even if you don't particularly like to do it.

Does he/she enjoy browsing in a flea market and you'd rather shop online? Try spending a weekend afternoon wandering through the flea market stalls with your partner and get excited when they find a treasure even if you think it's a piece of junk.

Your partner will appreciate the time you will have spent together and it will strengthen your relationship. The next outing could be one of your choices. Hopefully your partner will be as courteous as you were for their choices.

Entrepreneurial Thinking includes being respectful and considerate to other people. These positive actions are extremely important, especially to the significant other person in your life.

You should never take your spouse for granted. Instead, just pay attention to all their needs and desires. This is a sample of the Diamond Rule where you treat others the way they want to be treated.

Remember that if you're not careful, Relationships can be damaged by your actions.

Be aware that when your actions change. what started out as helpful reminders to your partner can sometimes cross the line into nagging or unconstructive criticism. Every now and then, complaining can degrade into constantly looking for what is wrong in your relationship rather than focusing on what is going well.

No one is really clairvoyant. Therefore, you shouldn't expect your partner to know how you are feeling or what you are expecting without your clearly communicating what you want.

When you're together, be together. Constantly checking your texts or staying on social media can cause a disconnect with your significant other. Agree ahead of time to turn off those electronics.

Similarly, bringing work from your office into your house can be a problem. If you must bring office work home, set a specific time frame to check your email or messages Set up a schedule like 7 to 8pm, then put your work away and focus on your family. You might even want to give your TV a rest a couple of nights a week.

First and foremost, you and your partner are on the same team. Friendly competition can be fun sometimes. However, if you are in a discussion, especially one that leads to an argument, handling the situation is delicate and needs practice to prevent confrontation.

While each person wants to be heard and understood, some mediation can be set up in advance. One family counselor suggests using a time frame like 5 minutes in which one person stated one opinion. Then, the other person also gets 5 minutes to present another opinion. During this time frame, the other person must remain quiet and attentive. In this way, at least the disagreement is mutually explained.

If this disagreement could potentially affect your relationship and if you feel that you must win, you will both lose. Your relationship over all should not rest on pettiness. The goal should be that "We can work it out peacefully." This goal needs to be more important than any petty problems or disagreements.

You should never let your own insecurities interfere with your relationship. This is especially true if you have trust issues based on previous relationships. Each person in a relationship should have the right to expect to be judged on what happens in this relationship, not be subjected to accusations based on the insecurities of the other person.

Do not feel defensive in your relationship. Defensiveness of one partner can quickly escalate even a fairly simple conversation into a conflict.

Entrepreneurial Thinking requires that you take responsibility for your own mistakes rather than making excuses or trying to blame someone else. This is critical in mistakes we make in relationships. Rather than get defensive when you know you messed up, take the heat, apologize, and move on to more important things. So, you forgot to pick up the laundry on the way home. Oops! My bad!

Okay, your partner messed up, big time! Don't constantly dredge up past mistakes just to make your partner feel guilty. While it's very tempting to relate current slip-ups to that thing that happened 8 years ago, you are just refueling a small fire. Try to forgive even if you cannot forget. Focus on what should be your ultimate goal – a happy, successful life. Having a good relationship is an ongoing process Relationships can be beautiful when you build them on your future rather than the dregs of the past.

For many reasons, keep most of your friends and all of social media out of your relationship. Some of your friends may simply be against long-term relationships. I had a co-worker one time who had been married and divorced several times. This person's solution to every little conflict between my wife and I was that we should split up and get divorced. Clearly, I should not have mentioned my marital concerns to this co-worker in the first place.

Your friends really don't understand all of the nuances of your relationship and will give you advice based their own insecurities and experience. Their life choices have no bearing on what your choices should be.

If you bash your partner on social media or trash them to your friends at the slightest provocation, the odds of possible reconciliation diminish significantly. It may be gratifying in the short term to try to garner support for your side of a situation, but again, if you feel that you must win, you both lose.

You must accept the fact that no one is perfect and no one is right 100% of the time, not even you. Therefore, you should always be caring and respectful towards your partner. The primary interaction that helps relationships last a very long time is mutual respect for each other.

When your partner provides you with a gift for a special occasion, always express your appreciation for the gift whether or not you think it is something you need. Also, If you are doing something that is not necessary like playing a video game and your significant other comes over to you to kind of cuddle up with you, it would be much better to positively respond to this affection rather than tell them that you feel a little interrupted or annoyed.

Honesty is the Best Policy – Mostly, but not always.

Obviously, you need to be honest with your partner about important things. Your partner needs to be able to trust in what you say. For example, you should be true to your partner. Fidelity is probably the single most important condition of a successful long-term relationship.

Be honest about finances. You shouldn't have secret bank accounts or charge cards that you use to keep your significant other in the dark about where your money goes. You both should agree on major purchases. If you have conflicting opinions about spending, you need to find a way to compromise. Financial conflicts are the second highest causes of divorce. The main cause of divorce is infidelity.

Sometimes though, being less than completely honest can actually strengthen your relationship. There are several situations when not being truthful will make your life and your relationship much better. Some people call them "little white lies."

Even if your partner's family really gets on your nerves, tell your partner how much you like them. If your partner tells you their family is coming to town for a visit, act the way your partner acts. If they're excited and happy then you should act the same way. You may have to grin and bear it, but it's worth it to keep harmony at home.

When your partner exercises their creativity in the kitchen and takes the time to prepare a meal, be grateful. Tell them that you really like their cooking. Unless you're afraid of getting ptomaine, keep any criticism to yourself.

Tell your partner how beautiful or good looking they are as often as they need to hear it. Mutual attraction brought you and your partner together in the first place. In any long-term relationship, things can change over time. The important thing is that your partner needs to be reassured that you still find them attractive and that you're not looking for any greener grasses.

When your partner is trying to make you laugh by telling a funny story, laugh at it. Even if their delivery is terrible or they forget the punchline, laugh anyway. Play along with them and give them the happiness they were trying to give to you. Besides, laughter is the best medicine.

When your partner comes home and is complaining about something that happened at work, listen without being critical or trying to fix it. Then when they tell you what they did, confirm that they did handled the situation well, even if you think your partner made a mistake. They are just venting about the problem and want a sympathetic ear. Allow your partner that opportunity without making suggestions. What if your partner tells you about issues at their job and asks your opinion about how they should respond? Remember that they probably should not act negatively while they are at work. Most likely, the best response would be to encourage your partner to work things out at their job site. If the situation is really terrible, then, perhaps, you may suggest that they try to find a different job, or even a different vocation.

In the earlier chapter about success the concept is that if a person is being treated unfairly, they can remove themselves from the situation and become successful in a different endeavor. Excessive stress at a job can cause illness. In any case, be supportive of your partner.

Realize that love is not a means to an end.

You should never use the love of another for you to manipulate that person. Having the love of another is a precious trust.

If you can, return the love to the person who loves you. If you can't, at least allow the Golden Rule to restrain your actions. Preferably, use the Diamond Rule.

You probably have seen relationships where one spouse is deeply in love and the other spouse has other motivations for the relationship. I knew a lady who had lost her husband in a terrible car wreck. She was the one driving and felt extremely guilty. The guilt feelings led to her finding solace in alcohol and she was an easy target for a man who had designs on her money.

She felt that she was in love with this new guy. They got married far too soon. He took advantage of her affection for him and took as much money away from her as he could as quickly as possible.

Then, just a few months after the marriage, he left her. She was terrified and lonely again but now she was also broke. Some people have no conscience. Clearly he did not respect his spouse, but he was using her love for him in order to steal almost all of her money.

The concept of taking advantage of persons who care about you is contrary to the concept of **Entrepreneurial Thinking.** As mentioned several times, Thinking like an Entrepreneur means to do the right thing at the right time for the correct reason.

Be more than a frog - Understanding Parenthood

Being a respectful adult has no relationship to simply having the biological ability to procreate. Even frogs have babies. Don't be a frog. Take responsibility for being a parent. The terms "Baby Mama" and "Baby Daddy" are insulting to the entire concept of parenthood.

The responsibility of being a mother doesn't end when you give birth to your child. Your responsibility started at the moment of conception and lasts for the remainder of your life or at least as long as your child lives.

Being a father, doesn't end when your sperm fertilizes the mother's egg. Your responsibility is to the mother of your child both during gestation and after the birth of your child. Your responsibility is to both mother and child for the remainder of your life or at least so long as they both live. Parenthood is a lifetime commitment for both Mother and Father. Don't take it lightly and abandon your child.

There have been multiple books and articles about parenthood and probably no parent can possibly read them all. Luckily, however, most of these books can be summed up in a few basic ideas.

First, you should be there when you are there. In other words, when you are spending time with your child, pay attention to your child. Being a responsible parent is accepting responsibility for your children; Financially, Physically, Emotionally, and Spiritually.

Financially: Parents need to be financially secure enough to take care of their children. This means that a parent needs to not be dependent on anyone else to financially take care of their child.

Physically and Emotionally: Parents need to be with their children as much as possible to nurture them as they grow. Children need to fully understand the fact that their parents will be around when they are needed. Children also need to fully understand that they are truly loved by their parents and that their parents will do their best to take care of their children for as long as necessary.

Spiritually: Parents need to provide a spiritual compass for their children whether or not the parents are significantly religious. Parents must help their children understand the necessity of being moral, ethical, honest, caring, and giving. Also, children need to be taught respect for themselves, their parents, and every other person they interact with.

Some parents encourage their children to be religious as spirituality is not innate. Parents have a duty to teach their offspring the basic of what is morally right and wrong. Morality is not a religion. Children have to be taught morality and ethics.

In the modern world where children are exposed at an early age to corruption, it is the parents who are responsible to limit exposure to inappropriate ideas. Parents can channel their offspring into age-appropriate culture.

Since the modern world with smart phones and easy viewing of hundreds of television shows and movies, parents must be on guard against ideas and pictures that challenge parental guidance; however, the observant parent can provide protection and guidance. Some restriction must be set as children are known to sometimes push the limits of many rules.

Children are naturally curious. It is one of the most sacred duties of parents to protect their children. Acceptable behavior should be taught at home not left to communities and schools. Parents have a responsibility to find out what their children are being exposed to or taught. Parenting is an active duty. Teachers continue to complain that the lack of discipline of school age children is mainly due to poor home training.

Setting rules and enforcing them is a duty. It is not cruel to restrict the actions of offspring. Many young people actually believe that no rules mean no love. By setting up and sticking to consequences of the actions of children, parents are preparing children for correct behavior, responsible goal setting, and goal setting that will last throughout their lives.

Behavioral science has shown that children's personality and highest period of learning take place before the age of six. Take advantage of the ability for children to learn during their early stages of life. Correction becomes more difficult with each passing year. You have probably heard stories of troubled teenagers that had no home guidance. Responsibility for actions is a key to entrepreneurial thinking and begins as soon as possible.

Punishment does not mean being cruel. The absence of television for a week is not being cruel. A pat on the bottom for a tiny toddler to remind the child not to play with matches may prevent a major situation in years to come. Cruelty is actual ignoring a problem and doing nothing to solve it. When a child comes to you for guidance, be honest and try to help.

Also, treat your child as you wanted to be treated when you were a child. Even better, treat them the way they want to be treated as long as it is reasonable. Specifically, be slow to anger and show the respect that even a child has the right to be listened to and to be understood.

Be sensitive to your child's feelings. You should never tell children that they "can't feel that way" when they are telling you how they feel. Instead try to understand why they feel that way and take steps to address their fears and concerns.

In a nurturing, safe home environment, children have a right to these five freedoms:

1. To see what they see and say it.
2. To hear what they hear and say it.
3. To feel what they feel and say it.
4. To want what they want and say it.
5. To think what they think and say it.

If a child's behavior is unacceptable, criticize the behavior, not the child. Parents should try to catch their children doing things the right way more than doing things the wrong way.

Striking your child in anger shows a lack of control on the part of the parent. Yes, children can be frustrating and there may be times when corporal punishment is warranted. This is especially true when the child is testing your resolve or challenging your decisions.

However, punishment must be reasonable and the child should know what behavior warranted the punishment. Children need to understand their boundaries.

When I was five years old, my best friend moved from next door to a house around the corner, across the alley. The rules were that I could not cross the street, even an alleyway, by myself. I knew when I sneaked down to my best friend's new house that I was breaking the rules.

When my father came looking for me, I tried, unsuccessfully, to hide under the table, behind some moving boxes. When he took me home, I received a painful swat on my butt and was sent to bed without supper. I knew that I deserved it. I did appreciate it when my mother brought me a snack. I resolved to never break the rules again.

Also, try to understand that babies come into the world full of life, love, and spontaneity. Nothing is more tragic than to see small children who have been scared so badly that they feel rotten about themselves. Parents must teach self-respect and responsibility. However, they also should instill self-confidence and self-reliance which are concepts in the benefit of thinking like an entrepreneur.

Responsible parenting may be the hardest job you will ever have. Children need parents to lead by example. You need to do the right thing, at the right time, for the right reason, in all situations.

Children learn how to treat others by the way they are treated. Your child is always watching you. Therefore, you need to be on your best behavior at all times. Children can learn to mimic their parents. They are small copy-cats. If mom or dad do certain things, then it must be all right for the children to do those things too.

The more you engage in the **Entrepreneurial Thinking** concepts of being considerate and doing the right thing at the right time for the right reason, the more your children will behave properly.

Parents need to hug their children, especially if they come asking or if you recognize that they need it. Every human being has an innate need for the non-aggressive, non-sexual touch of another human being. Although teaching them the importance of good touch bad touch is as important as not running off from strangers, children should be able to hug or be hugged and know the difference between being greeted and being assaulted.

Parents, guardians, family, and friends should never withhold affection as a punishment. Parental love should be unconditional even when poor behavior needs correction. Love the child; dislike the poor behavior.

Personal interaction is important.

Be willing to give your loved ones a hug, especially when they need it. Be willing to ask for a hug when you need it. Asking for a hug is not a sign of weakness, but, rather, an acceptance of your humanity. All normal humans require the positive, supportive, caring, non-sexual touch of another human being.

Our current focus on teaching, "good touch-bad touch" is creating a generation of children who are sometimes afraid of being touched at all. It is also creating parents, grandparents, aunts and uncles, who are afraid of showing affection to the children in their life.

One has to wonder what the result will be in the future of this tendency not to hug. It could be that in the not-too-distant future, individuals will become even more isolated and unable to relate to people around them.

In fact, there have been several studies recently about how smart phones and social media systems like Facebook, Instagram, Twitter, and others are causing people who are together to actually disconnect from each other. Many times, being face-down in your smart phone can cause you to ignore the people you are actually with. There have been cartoons showing a dating couple at a restaurant communicating with each other by texting rather than talking.

It is polite to actually listen to somebody who is talking to you in person. Only a rude person would focus on their electronic devise when live people are taking their good tome to spend with you.

If you think that it is more important to check that Facebook notification you just received to see what's up with your friend across town or across the country, then at least stay home alone to do so.

You should always pay more attention to the person sitting next to you at the table who is talking to you. Besides it is polite to actually listen to somebody who is talking to you in person.

Thinking like an Entrepreneur means treating others at least like you would want to be treated, but more importantly, like they want to be treated. So, be courteous and polite and connect more with the person you are actually with in person.

You must be where you are in your body and mind while you pay attention to the people around you. When you are at work, be at work and do what you are being paid to do rather than spend time worrying about what might be happening at your home. When you are at home, spend time with your loved ones and do tasks that will make your home better rather than spend all your time thinking about your workplace.

Listen to your heart.

Your heart will tell you if the object of your affection is someone you want to spend your life with. Make sure it is your heart you are listening to and not a more selfish body part.

Likewise, especially at first, be aware of any red flags that your significant other is exhibiting. Does that person seem to be too controlling? Do you feel like the relationship is one-sided? Are you already being criticized? Is the other person negative with no optimism? Is your friend focused only on money or fame?

Listen to your heart, for sure, but also listen to your gut if prince or princess charming starts behaving like the wicked witch of the west. Like any person with whom you have a relationship, the other person should treat you the way you want to be treated. You should do the same by treating them the way they want to be treated.

Obviously, neither of you is a mind-reader, but one must always be polite even if it tries your patience.

Negativity and conflict from another person should never be accepted or tolerated. Also, if you expect respect and tolerance yourself, you should not be negative or engage in conflict either.

Be assured that you and your partner are on the same team. Friendly competition might be OK on game night, but not when you're making decisions that impact your relationship. Think before you act or speak. Keep in mind that once out of your mouth, words cannot be breathed back in. Apologies are just words. Sometimes you will be better off just being quiet. Silence may not solve the situation, but you will have fewer regrets later.

Another behavior that couples need to alter is thinking that their partner knows everything about them without being told. Your partner can't read your mind. You need to communicate clearly about your needs and concerns so that your partner will understand how to respond. In good relationships, partners are honest and assertive about expressing their needs, and preferences. Their partners are the same way.

For instance, if you like or dislike a certain food, make it known. If you are allergic to any foods, it would be good to explain why you cannot eat certain things. Some allergies are so bad that you can have to go to the emergency room if you eat the wrong thing. This kind of communication is very necessary to keep the relationship mutually beneficial.

Understand Love.

Understand that love is giving and sharing, supporting and caring. Love is waiting instead of hurrying; listening rather than talking. Love is forgiving instead of holding a grudge; celebrating instead of envying. Love is not selfish and controlling.

Obsession and stalking are also not love but a form of mental abuse. Sending cutesy texts may seem like a good idea. It is a good idea to strengthen your relationship to a point. However, by sending cutesy texts hundreds of times a day you could have slipped from love into negative obsession and abuse by trying to control the actions of your partner all day long.

You may feel like you are simply strongly expressing your love. However, being too aggressive, abusive, and controlling of your partner can damage the relationship. Make sure that you do not mistake another emotion for love or you might find a restraining order keeping you from your imagined true love.

Thinking like an Entrepreneur always includes being courteous and considerate.

Tell your loved ones that you love them every day.

Life if short and if we miss the opportunity to tell our loved ones how much they mean to us, we might regret it for years.

I was 21 years old, working full time and going to college at night, living at home with my mother and father. My father had had a stroke and had been out of work for many months. I, being the dutiful son that I was, was giving over half my salary to my parents for room and board.

I had been out late with my girlfriend the night before and was struggling to get out of bed that morning.

My father came in several times to tell me to get up so I could get ready to go to work and the last time he came in I was pretty irritated. I kind of raised my voice and said, "Ok, Daddy, I'll get up in a minute."

I kind of laid back down for a few minutes and drifted back to sleep. Then I heard a loud thump in the other part of the house. I was kind of disoriented but I heard my mother cry out like something was wrong. I jumped out of bed, pulled on my pants and ran into the living room.

There was my father, lying on the floor, unconscious and my mother was clearly distraught and was barely leaning over him. I tried mouth to mouth resuscitation and all I heard was the air I had blown into his lungs rattle on the way out. I listened to his heart trying to hear any sounds of life but did not hear a heartbeat. I tried CPR but there was no response. He was dead.

My father was dead. This loving man who had saved my life when I had a piece of hard candy stuck in my throat and couldn't breathe, when I was 10 years old, was gone. This caring man who cried when I left home because I was drafted by the army was gone. This gentle father who used to carry me on his shoulders to watch the parades downtown was dead. Did I tell him how much I loved him? Not recently and not nearly enough! The last words I said to him were curt and irritated.

Each of us only have limited time and we never know how important one day is until it's gone. Take the time today to express your affection and appreciation to the significant people in your life.

This is one of the tenants of **Entrepreneurial Thinking**: do what needs to be done when it needs to be done rather than do things only when you get around to doing them. Don't put this off today because you may regret it tomorrow.

Chapter Nine

Embrace Your Creativity

Nourish your creativity.

Whatever your talent is, spend time cultivating it. You need to spend at least an hour a day working with your creativity. Failure to do this can lead to depression, despair, and a belief in the futility of life.

Everyone has some talent. However, not everyone is aware of exactly what their talent is. Even when you are talented, if you don't take the time to try, you might never understand what you are capable of.

Be spontaneous; not careless.

When you have the opportunity for some unstructured time, make sure it is spent doing something you really enjoy. Keep your overall goals in mind, but take the time to branch out into other pursuits if only for the experience.

Do things that are exciting and different. Get out of your comfort zone. Just make certain that you don't do anything stupid like bungee jumping off your 12' garage with a 15' bungee cord and crashing onto your driveway.

Consider that you might want to learn to play a musical instrument.

You will feel immense satisfaction when you play, even if it is just for your own pleasure. The discipline it takes for you to learn such a skill will translate into the ability to concentrate on any endeavor in life and will enhance your sense of self-worth.

Instruments can sometimes be rented from local music stores. Try one or two before buying any. After acquiring an instrument, consider taking lessons.

Entrepreneurial Thinking requires the ability to focus on tasks until completion. Just remember that practice doesn't make perfect, practice makes permanent. If you practice over and over the wrong way to do something you will never improve. This is why you need a mentor or coach to keep you practicing the correct way.

The same holds true for learning any new skill. Whether you are learning to play an instrument or learning a new business, try to find a mentor who has accomplished what you want to do. Learn from them. You shouldn't think that you need to try to reinvent the wheel when you can learn how to do it from someone who can help you. If a fee is charged, think of it as a payment for the future of yourself.

Learn to appreciate the artistic endeavors of others.

Go to see a live production of a play. Go to a symphonic or pops concert, or attend a music festival. Visit an art gallery or museum.

Whether or not your talent is in any one of these fields, you need to understand what it takes to accomplish these feats of creativity. In this way you at least will learn to respect the artists and the art.

By being impressed with these artists, you might become inspired to attempt some of these endeavors yourself and find an undiscovered talent. The more you spend the time to appreciate other people's artistic abilities, the more likely you will consider doing something similar for your own personal accomplishments.

Thinking like an Entrepreneur includes taking steps to improve your life every day. Therefore, even if you were not inspired to attempt to become a professional artist, your visit to the art gallery was still probably very enjoyable and entertaining.

Log your creativity.

Keep a diary, log book, or digital recorder close at hand so that if you have an idea, you can record it when you have it. Nothing is more frustrating than trying to remember that idea you had last night, and that now you simply can't remember what it was. You know it was brilliant, it could make you rich, and it could be a benefit to all of mankind, if you could just remember what it was. Dang it!

Many successful entrepreneurs keep a note pad or recording device nearby where they are, including their bed, so that if they have a brilliant idea, they can make a record of it before they forget it.

Dr. James Watson, one of the early pioneers of DNA research had been working on trying to figure out the structure of the DNA molecule. He went to sleep thinking about the problem and dreamed about two intertwined snakes with heads on opposite ends. When he woke up he immediately wrote down what he had been dreaming about and realized he had dreamed the solution to the structure of the DNA molecules he had been trying to figure out. Fortunately, after he wrote it down, he became famous for his design of the DNA structure.

Along with the idea of logging your creativity, the obvious next step is to keep a journal of your life.

You don't need to write something every day, but you should write frequently enough so that as you age, you can look back and understand who you were in different stages of your life. This journal should NOT be on Facebook, Twitter, Instagram or any other social media site. You do not need to make every move you make public.

You also don't want prospective employers or potential lovers to know about how your obsession with your 8th grade English teacher led you to be arrested for stalking when you were 15. Most bad decisions you make should be kept to yourself.

To add emphasis to the importance of keeping things to yourself just read some of what happens when people share too much. Recently a teenager was live streaming herself on facebook driving drunk and filmed the wreck she was in. She left the scene of the accident, but was tracked down because of her live streaming on Facebook. The result was that she will spend significant time in jail. This is an extreme example.

Consider making your journal mostly about positive occurrences throughout your life. You can mention things that shaped your character or caused a major trauma. As a means of airing the issue, make sure you don't dwell on the negative. You don't want to be reading your journal later in life which is filled with nothing but terrible memories. Remembering all of the bad things could cause depression, which is already a problem for many senior citizens.

If you haven't started a journal yet, you can begin it with a few Memory Joggers. First, get a physical journal to write in. Then check out a few of these Memory Joggers to get started:

1. Tell about the houses you lived in while you were growing up, especially where they were located and the type of house they were.

2. Tell about your mother, her personality, stature, talents, and her role in your family. Then, using specific occurrences, describe your relationship with your mother from your first memories until you left home,

3. Do the same for your father.

4. Describe your relationships with your grandparents. Discuss how they affected your life and add family stories regarding them.

5. Write about aunts and uncles, or other relatives that you spent a lot of time with. Write about their influence on you but primarily focus on positivity.

6. Write about your siblings, if you had any that you lived with as a child. Focus on the positive.

Describe fun family times like vacations, social events and your quiet times.

7. Finally, write about yourself. Were there any strange insider stories about your birth and early childhood? Discuss who chose your name and why it was chosen for you?

8. Describe your school days and school friends, especially when you were successful and have happy memories about the times. Describe the different ways you acted as you grew up in each of the time periods such as elementary school to high school

9. Jot down memories of any serious illnesses or accidents that changed any portions of your life. If things like this happened, how did you survive and recuperate to have a better life after their occurrences?

10. Write about the most significant world or local event that has happened so far during your lifetime and if so, explain how the event effected you.

11. Did you have any vacations or adventures that made an impression on you like going to camp or on a school trip? Include the events that you might have participated in if you spent time as either a girl scout or a boy scout.

12. Write about other people who were helpful such as neighbors, teachers, church members, or

community leaders. Other choices are perhaps, playground attendants, ice cream truck drivers, or store clerks.

Other ideas that will help you remember your positive memories of your past are perhaps games you won as a child, people you met in the past who were helpful, as well as how much fun you used to have playing outside.

In the end, your perception of your life will be the total sum of the memories you made and can recall. Keep good notes as you go along. Like everyone else, you only pass through life once.

Perhaps writing about your passing through life will help you to realize that time is the only completely non-renewable resource that you have. If you go broke, you can always theoretically find another way to make some money. If your relationship terminates, whether or not it was your fault, you can usually find another person that you could possibly develop a good relationship with. However, if you actually completely run out of time you're gone. One of the tenants of **Entrepreneurial Thinking** is to make good use of your time on a daily basis.

As an example of remembering your past, here is a letter I wrote a few years ago to my deceased father:

Dear Daddy:
I think that this is the first letter I ever wrote to you. I want to say "Thank you" for giving me life and for setting a wonderful example of how to be a good person. I never

saw you drink too much. You were never abusive to any of us kids or to Mama. You showed me how to be a caring, loving person who was always willing to lend a helping hand. You used to take me to several relatives that were so poor, you were the one who brought them groceries once a week. You may not have been perfect, but I know that you always did the best you could for everyone in our family.

I am very also happy that my fiancée got to meet you and spend some time with you before you passed away. She loved you very much and was grateful for your acting as her father as well.

I love you and have missed you for many years. I hope to see you in heaven.

Love,
Your Son,
Edward

Take an intense adventure rather than a relaxing vacation.

Every so often you need to shake things up to expand who you are and what you know. Rather than take another vacation week off and simply sit around at the beach again, go take a mountain climbing class or perhaps a survival training course. Consider that you could learn to ski, to go horseback riding, paddle a canoe, go scuba diving or snorkeling.

When you accomplish a new task or learn a new skill, you will come back stronger, healthier, and more knowledgeable. You will also potentially become more confident of your abilities to tackle new tasks.

Since unshakable self-confidence is one of the hallmarks of **Entrepreneurial Thinking**. Anything you can do to increase your self-confidence is something you should seriously consider doing.

Chapter Ten

Taking The High Road
Is Being Ethical

Be the better person.

Ethical behavior is characterized by trustworthiness, fairness and impartiality in personal and professional relationships. Ethical behavior respects the dignity and rights of all individuals whether in personal or business relationships.

In every situation in life, be slow to judge. Never be petty or vindictive. Always make decisions from a higher perspective than personal gain. Personal gain may be a goal, but it should not ever cause pain and suffering to another person.

Ethical behavior is a significant part of **Entrepreneurial Thinking**. Whenever possible, all results should be focused on becoming a Win-Win situation for everyone involved.

In order for any situation to become Win-Win, all persons involved should understand and agree that Win-Win is the best alternative. Win-Lose will always cause vindictiveness and conflict and should be avoided whenever possible.

Always be ethical

Historically speaking, the word ethical comes from the Greek word "ethos." Ethos means "moral character" which describes a person or behavior which is in positive morality, sensitivity, truthfulness, fairness, and honesty.

Ethics are what you do when no one is watching you or checking up on you. The Golden Rule is the most well-known example of ethical behavior.

However, the Diamond Rule is probably much more important. You usually need to treat people the way they want to be treated.

Entrepreneurial Thinking involves the need to develop a personal code of ethics that you can follow throughout your life. This code will help you make the correct choices in all decisions that can affect yourself and all others you are in relationships with.

In a service business, you need to do what is best for your clients. This way you will have clients that will refer you to other potential clients. They also will encourage these other people to use you for the service you are providing.

In a personal setting, being ethical will garner more respect and keep people near you to care about you because you are a good person. You can't buy this kind of respect. It needs to be earned by doing the right thing at the right time for the right reason at all times.

Ethical behavior makes our society harmonious and peaceful. Therefore, by guiding the behavior of people, our society becomes a better place to live. Ethics essentially is a self-governing system that keeps the good of society at equilibrium with human self-interest.

Your personal ethical behavior can be affected by your knowledge, your personal goals, your personality, and your moral beliefs. The best way to stay ethical is to believe in the importance of consistently doing the right thing at the right time for the right reason. Doing this should done regardless of any other social factors or cultural norms that may be negative to ethical behavior.

Being ethical is doing what we ought to do. If we are ethical, we will consistently treat others with kindness, compassion, respect, and etcetera. In other words, if you are an ethical person, you will practice applying virtues to your character traits, for making everyday decisions.

Find solutions to conflicts.

Always try to find the solution to a problem rather than try to point your finger at who might be at fault. This is especially true if the one at fault might be you.

The bottom line is to find the solution to a problem in order to resolve any negative effects that the problem has created. By working on finding a solution to a problem rather than trying to blame anyone else, you will find the solution more rapidly. Finding the correct solution should be the primary goal in order to positively correct the problem.

Always be Reliable.

Just do what you say you will do when you say you will do it. **Entrepreneurial Thinking** assumes that anyone who interacts with you can be certain of your reliability.

Reliability is especially true in regards to business contacts that can benefit your financial well-being. However, in personal dealings, reliability will always improve your relationships. You will need to be there to help your family and friends when they need assistance.

In Every Situation, Strive to Be the Peacemaker.

Whether you are in a personal or professional setting, you will sometimes occasionally find yourself in the middle of conflicts of one type or another. Other people may be trying to elicit your support for whatever cause or concern they are backing.

Do not let yourself be drawn into any argument. Ask questions and try to calm the situation. Then make suggestions to the persons having the conflict that will help them to reduce their negativity and consider potential compromises. In some cases, you man need to step away or you may become part of the problem you were trying to solve.

Expect most people to make every mistake once.

In any relationship, sometimes misunderstandings can occur. Mistakes can be made through lack of communication or lack of skill.

Sometimes, people tend to be mistaken because they don't understand the response you are trying to get from them. If a person does make a mistake one time, give them a second chance to respond properly and correct their error. Do not give them a third chance to continue to make the same mistake. Three of the same mistakes by the same person, typically indicates either a character flaw or failure in the skill of the person you are trying to instruct.

If the person refuses to follow directions, that person may not be teachable in that area. With that many mistakes that should have been corrected, it might indicate that the person is perhaps either are too arrogant to follow guidelines, or too ignorant to follow directions. The other probability is that perhaps they are too careless or lazy to want to follow your instructions.

One of the consistent tenants of optimistic **Entrepreneurial Thinking** requires that you keep positive people in your inner circle as much as possible.

Negativity, especially from anyone you relate to on a consistent basis can cause you to second-guess your goals. Similarly, such negativity can reduce your vision as well as impede your progress. This is why you need to try to improve your relationships with people who respond positively to you and their environment.

When necessary, be critical, but not harsh.

Giving positive criticism is your goal. Criticism should be used only when suggesting a change in the process that would make the solution better. Being critical should never be to just try to find fault with another person. Constructive criticism should be used with a genuine intent to help. The purpose should never be to try to make the other person feel bad about themselves. Explain that your efforts are to help them improve for their benefits.

You should always save your strongest negative criticism for yourself. This focus on internal negativity should only be an incentive for you to strive to do better. Simply beating yourself up is counter-productive. Remember that you cannot undo the past, you can only improve the present and the future.

Entrepreneurial Thinking is avoiding negativity. Find solutions that will improve your activities and benefit your life. Do not dwell on the past; yet learn from your failures. Remember that thinking like Thomas Edison, if you have a failure, you have simply learned one less way of finding the solution. Again, thinking outside the box implies that you will take whatever steps that are necessary to improve what you are trying to accomplish.

Never worry about things you cannot control.

Either do something to resolve any problem that you have or simply try to forget about it. My grandmother told me, "Worry never takes the unhappiness out of tomorrow, it just takes the happiness out of today." Besides, worry is simply the fear about what might happen in the future. Feeling that a specific event in the future will be negative is called catastrophizing.

The whole idea of the future is that it basically is mostly unknown. Since the future is mostly unknown, you should save your concern for things that happen that you know about. Basically, focus on being proactive in your life rather than wasting time and energy worrying about things that you can't control.

According to Grand Master OOgway in the movie, Kung Fu Panda, "Yesterday is history, Tomorrow is a mystery, but today is a Gift. That is why it is called the Present."

You really shouldn'tworry about anything that you don't know about yet. According to Zig Ziglar, "Worry is negative goal setting."

Whatever is worrying you the most, simply write it down. Next, write down what you can currently do about what your concerns are. Perhaps, even GOOGLE the solution if it helps you to find out how others did what you are trying to do. The key is to find a solution. You will solve nothing by wasting your time worrying about it.

By seeking help, you might find a solution, so that you can realize that your worries were about nothing that you should have worried about. Choose the method you think will work for you and take action immediately.

One of the basic ideas of the law of attraction is that you attract what you think about. Using this concept, the more you worry about specific things, the more likely it becomes that those things that you are fearful of will find their way into your life.

Change the things you can. Accept the things you can't change. This is the Serenity Prayer: "God Grant me the **Serenity** to accept the things I cannot change; the **Courage** to change the things I can and the **Wisdom** to know the difference."

Entrepreneurial Thinking entails a modification to the Serenity Prayer. This version is as follows: "God Grant me the **Courage** to change the things I can; the **Wisdom** to know when it's time to stop trying because what I was trying to change is beyond my ability to change it and; finally, give me the **Serenity** to accept the things I cannot change."

There is an old song entitled "Que Sera Sera." In the song it says, "Whatever will be will be, The future's not ours to see, Que Sera Sera." However, **thinking like an entrepreneur** means that you have to give everything you want to accomplish your best attempt.

Any goal that you believe is important enough to set for yourself needs to be pursued with vigor and purpose. Don't give up unless you have no other choice.

Be inspirational to others.

You may think that no one is watching you, but someone always is. Consistently set a good example. In any public environment, look over your shoulder and you will probably see someone out of the corner of your eye that you didn't notice. This is not to make you paranoid but to use as an example of people who might be influenced by you.

Make sure that what you are doing is positive and productive. Give praise and recognition to everyone who deserves it. Undeserved praise is hollow and insults the intelligence of the recipient.

The recent tendency for children to be presented awards for simply showing up rather than actually excelling in any endeavor could affect their willingness to try to succeed throughout their life. **Entrepreneurial thinking** means that one understands the importance of hard work in order to accomplish critical tasks towards meaningful goals.

Try to be observant to your surroundings.

You don't need to be Sherlock Holmes to notice your surroundings and how other people behave. To **think like an Entrepreneur**, you will need to be acutely aware of what is going on around you at all times.

You will never know when you might become aware of an opportunity that could benefit you either now or in the future. You might notice someone else doing something that you could incorporate into your life.

Perhaps you will notice a product or service that you might be able to modify in order to generate additional income. If you see someone doing something that you find worthwhile, then pay attention. At some point you should decide if it is something that would benefit you if you were to start doing something similar.

The similar enterprise may be beneficial, but like all endeavors, you will still need a plan. As with all plans, you will need to make certain that you are able to take all the necessary steps to become successful.

Look for the good in all people.

Everyone deserves the chance to earn your respect and acceptance. If they are honest and grateful then they may earn such respect. If they make good with their attitude and abilities, they might become friends.

On the other hand, if they profess goodness but perform suspiciously, you need to realize that not everyone has as much good within themselves as they claim.

Once someone has shown their true harmful colors, do not give them a chance to negatively affect you or your family. As always, **Entrepreneurial Thinking** encourages you to keep positive people in your inner circle and keep negative pcople away

Be aware that you can't please everyone; don't try to.

All you can do at any moment is to try to do the finest you can do. If that doesn't please everyone, it has nothing to do with you. However, you need to be completely honest with yourself that you are, in fact, doing the absolutely greatest thing you can in what you are undertaking.

Simply professing that you are doing the best you can do is not the same thing as actually doing the best you can do. Again, **Entrepreneurial Thinking** entails taking the necessary steps to complete whatever goal you are attempting to accomplish in the correct manner. Therefore, as you actually do accomplish your goal, you don't need to worry about anyone else's reaction to it. It is more important for you to be successful for yourself

Be conscious of how other people react to you.

You should always strive to be approachable and friendly. You want people to be comfortable around you. **Entrepreneurial Thinking** requires that you always appear to be a positive, trustworthy person because this is the type of person you truly are.

If you sense that people avoid you, maybe it is because you appear distant or unfriendly in some way. You don't need to grovel or be subservient in an attempt to give the impression that you are sociable. Sometimes the "in things to do" is not correctly thinking like an entrepreneur.

You should always be perceived as someone who people can easily interact with. The more comfortable people feel when they are around you, the more likely they will be willing to assist you in accomplishing your goals. Usually having others to assist you in accomplishing your goals will be very helpful for you to do so. Popularity may be helpful but be careful what you are popular for. You may want to stand out in a crowd, but you don't want people to think you are a psychopath.

Smile.

Yes, smile, even when you don't feel like it, smile anyway. It will improve your looks and the way others respond to you. Eventually smiling will improve your own mood. As stated earlier in the book, a Smile is understood in every language on earth and it is a very good ice breaker when you meet anyone. Therefore, the more you smile every day, the better you will feel and the better other people will treat you.

Don't isolate yourself.

Other people can be a source of inspiration, amusement, and sometimes financial gain. You are not an island but part of the family of humankind. The more you have associations with others, the more likely you will have the opportunities to expand your ability to generate additional income. This is possible but not necessarily guaranteed.

As you embrace the association of others, be a little bit wary. Even the best of friends can sometimes become an enemy without you even knowing why.

Once I started a business with one of my best childhood friends. As the business progressed, my friend decided that because I was the principal financier of the business, he had the right to take advantage of the business. While we were remodeling the facility, he stole building supplies and remodeled his house. Finally, several months after the business was generating monthly income, he stole the total monthly income. This caused me to have to close the business and go bankrupt. This is an example of how important it is to only have positive people interact with you on a consistent basis.

Be respectful to your parents.

Entrepreneurial Thinking requires respect for everyone you encounter until they do something to invalidate your respect for them. Your parents are the first and foremost people that you should respect for your entire life. They had a life before you were born and will have a life again when you move out. Their world only seems to revolve around you because they are patiently waiting for you to become a responsible adult. Don't be one of the **KIPPERS**. **K**ids in **P**arents **P**ockets **E**roding **R**etirement **S**avings.

Care for others and offer help.

Consider that caring is not weakness. It is, in fact, one of the hallmarks of our humanity. There is an old saying, "No man stands as tall as he does when he stoops to helps a child." This concept applies to helping anyone else who is worse off than you are.

According to Star Trek, the three words that are the most important in relationships are "Let me help" rather than "I love you."

Be patient.

Have patience with animals and small children; they are probably both smarter than you think they are.

Have patience with the elderly. They know more than you think they do. They deserve your respect and honor. The simple fact that they are much older than you means that they have more experience in life. More experience in living provides more knowledge and understanding.

Be responsible for the care of your pets.

If you have a pet, you have assumed the responsibility for another life. Animals give us unconditional love and companionship. It is our charge to give back care and compassion. You must never abuse, or neglect an animal. They are dependent on you for food, warmth, positive contact, and medical care.

The true measure of our humanity is found in how we care for animals in our trust. Pets are not disposable even if they belong to someone else.

When I was very young, two neighborhood boys, both of whom were 6 to 7 years older than I, would sometimes kill very small stray kittens for fun. It was like a "Silence Of The Lambs" moment. I was horrified at such cruelty and vowed to protect animals for the rest of my life.

In fact, once I learned that the County commissioner was being presented with complaints about feral cat colonies. I went to the meeting and presented a methodology that could reduce the numbers of abandoned kittens that had to live in these colonies with spay, neuter, and return. The manager of the local humane society told me that she wished more people were like me to help protect animals.

Clearly, hurting animals that typically are pets is not a good thing to do. To do so, you will be judges as a very cruel person. Such cruelty and negativity is mostly counterproductive. One of the tenants of **Entrepreneural Thinking** is to never be counterproductive no matter what the behavior entails.

Be carefully generous.

BE generous with your time and money. Just remember that charity begins at home. Be aware that every great philanthropist first had to amass a great fortune before becoming extremely generous.

Despite the magnanimous generosity of the Bill Gates foundation today, rumors of the cutthroat tactics of Microsoft in the early days still haunt the internet.

Assuming you will probably never be nearly as rich as some billionaire, you will need to be cautiously generous. Give from your heart, but make sure that you do not give away your ability to pay your bills. Investigate charities to make sure that the primary beneficiaries of the charity are not the people who run it.

Be especially wary of any charity that advertises heavily on television or makes unsolicited phone calls to you. The odds are that most of their resources go to advertising and administration costs rather than to the causes they claim to benefit.

When I was running the Fort Screven Preservation Society, a non-profit organization trying to protect 19th century coastal fortifications, I received many phone calls and letters offering assistance for my fund-raising goals. Each of these offers included an agreement that the fund-raising organization would be allowed to keep from 50% to 75% of the funds that they received from donors as compensation for their marketing campaign.

Of course, I refused because I wanted any donations received to go to save the historical structures rather than pay the advertising companies. Potentially, many non-profit organizations today actually pay other companies as part of their fund-rasing and administration costs.

Fifteen Simple Positive Thoughts.

1. The best way to go anywhere is to start.
2. Every journey starts with a first step.
3. The Perfect moment to start is Now.
4. Change "I Wish" to "I Will."
5. Add more Smiles to your Day.
6. Create your own brightness.
7. Think "Yes I Can."
8. Find the positive in all things.
9. Every Day gives you a New Opportunity.
10. Be Happy for Your life.
11. Be grateful for everything in your life.
12. Let no one rain on your parade
13. Be the blossom in the rain
14. You Got This.
15. Be your Best Today and Everyday.

Epilogue

These guidelines should give every person some insight of what it takes to be successful in their life. Some of these concepts of **Entrepreneurial Thinking** are combinations of personal experience and learned concepts of self-mastery. Other concepts include common sense and respect.

If you follow these guidelines to the best of your ability, you will have a much happier life. Also, you will potentially be much better off physically and financially. By using these strategies as suggested, most everyone you meet will find you to be a true friend, honest husband or wife, esteemed colleague, and respected member of our society.

I hope these ideas will plant the seeds of decency, honesty, and a respect for yourself and others because without mutual respect, our society will collapse under the strain of greed, corruption, and hostility.

Entrepreneurial Thinking can help you to **Win At Life** by succeeding today, tomorrow, and for the rest of your life.

Author's Biography

Edward L. Cawley was born in Savannah, Georgia. He received his BBA degree in Information Systems from Armstrong State College in Savannah. He worked as a senior computer programmer, systems analyst, and data processing liaison for corporate acquisitions in corporate America. In his governmental position, he was a district manager of information systems and the State Network administrator for 27 southeastern Georgia Counties.

As an entrepreneur, he opened the first group personal care home in Savannah Georgia. In an effort to broaden his understanding of health, he took over 30 hours towards a Masters of Health Science Degree. This additional education helped him learn how to get healthier and to take better care of the residents in the personal care facility.

As a real estate investor and developer, he purchased profitable property for many years. He also obtained his real estate license. He purchased and then sold rental property for a substantial profit. He also built a spec house and developed vacant land for residential construction.

Additionally, he founded the Fort Screven Preservation Society, a non-profit corporation that was working to preserve coastal fortifications from the late 19th Century on Tybee Island, Georgia.

Mr. Cawley has also been a licensed financial services professional for over 20 years.

Avocational pursuits included years of dramatic studies and on-stage performances in community theater, musical studies and compositions, as well as a lifelong love of the written word.

His education, vocations and avocations run a lifelong gamut of knowledge and experience. Because of his broad expanse of knowledge and experience, he is an excellent example of what it truly means to be a Renaissance Man.

He is one of those heroes who found a job and worked to support his family for many years, while putting his own dreams on hold. Now he is endeavoring to complete a few of his dreams before he says goodbye to this world.

He currently lives with his wife, Florence Cawley who he has been married with for over 53 years and several cats on Tybee Island, Georgia.

Jacket notes.

Through his years in leadership positions and his participation in personal and professional development, Ed Cawley has established a unique set of guidelines that should help readers understand how to become successful, improve their finances, their self-confidence, their overall abilities, their health, their relationships, their creativity, and their ethics as well as hopefully instilling a sense of humanity and humility and desire to improve our society.

Entrepreneurial Thinking, How Thinking Like An Entrepreneur can help you Win At Life, is a meaningful guide to improving every facet of your life. Yet, it has a partially lighthearted touch that can sometimes make you smile when you least expect it.

Certificate of Registration

This Certificate issued under the seal of the Copyright
Office in accordance with title 17, *United States Code,*
attests that registration has been made for the work
identified below. The information on this certificate has
been made a part of the Copyright Office records.

Shira Perlmutter

United States Register of Copyrights and Director

Registration Number

TXu 2-375-243

Effective Date of Registration:
June 22, 2023
Registration Decision Date:
June 22, 2023

Copyright Registration for One Work by One Author
Registration issued pursuant to 37 CFR §202.3

Title

Title of Work:	Entrepreneurial Thinking - How Thinking Like an Entrepreneur Can Help You "Win At Life"

Completion/Publication

Year of Completion:	2023

Author

Author:	Ed Cawley
Author Created:	Nonfiction Work
Citizen of:	United States
Year Born:	1947

Copyright Claimant

Copyright Claimant:	Ed Cawley
	P.O. Box 279, Tybee Island, GA, 31328, United States

Certification

Name:	Ed Cawley, Author/Owner
Date:	May 18, 2023

Correspondence:	Yes
Copyright Office notes:	Regarding basis for registration: A work may be registered with the Single Application only if the following requirements have been met: 1) The registration covers one work; 2) The work must be created by one individual; 3)